Kindness

Kindness

Change your life and make the world a kinder place

Gill Hasson

CAPSTONE
A Wiley Brand

This edition first published 2018

© 2018 Gill Hasson

Registered office
John Wiley & Sons Ltd, The Atrium, Southern Gate, Chichester, West Sussex, PO19 8SQ, United Kingdom

For details of our global editorial offices, for customer services and for information about how to apply for permission to reuse the copyright material in this book please see our website at www.wiley.com.

Gill Hasson has asserted her right under the Copyright, Designs and Patents Act, 1988, to be identified as the author of this Work.

Library of Congress Cataloging-in-Publication Data

Names: Hasson, Gill, author.
Title: Kindness : change your life and make the world a kinder place / by Gill Hasson.
Description: Hoboken, NJ ; Chichester, UK : John Wiley & Sons, 2018. | Includes index. |
Identifiers: LCCN 2018003945 (print) | ISBN 9780857087522 (pbk.)
Subjects: LCSH: Kindness. | Conduct of life.
Classification: LCC BJ1533.K5 (ebook) | LCC BJ1533.K5 H37 2018 (print) | DDC 177/.7–dc23
LC record available at https://lccn.loc.gov/2018003945

A catalogue record for this book is available from the British Library.

ISBN 978-0-857-08752-2 (pbk)
ISBN 978-0-857-08767-6 (ebk)
ISBN 978-0-857-08766-9 (ebk)

Cover Design: Wiley

Set in 12/15pt SabonLTStd by Aptara Inc., New Delhi, India
Printed in Great Britain by TJ International Ltd, Padstow, Cornwall, UK

10 9 8 7 6 5 4 3 2 1

*To my grandmother Yιαγιά Lily and her sister,
my great aunt, Theía Litsa.*

Contents

Introduction

We are all here on earth to help others; what on earth the others are here for I don't know.

comedian John Foster Hall, quoted by W. H. Auden

We need more kindness!

It's easy to think that bad things happen in the world all the time; a continual stream of headlines describing all sorts of horrors and wrongdoings can keep us in a near permanent state of worry and mistrust. Sometimes it can feel like everyone's out to get each other. Having to deal with constantly horrifying news is not good for any of us. But what, if anything, can you do about it all?

In his book *The Seven Habits of Highly Effective People*, Stephen Covey explains the concept of the 'Circle of Concern' and the 'Circle of Influence'. The Circle of Concern is the area that we have no control over but that we often spend time and energy getting caught up in; getting wound up and worried about.

A wide range of events – the economy, war and terrorism, the behaviour of celebrities, sports stars and politicians, for example – fall into the Circle of Concern. You have little or no control over these events, but you can easily consume more and more information about them. It drains your time and energy and can leave you feeling stressed, helpless and negative simply *because* you have little or no control over these events.

The Circle of Influence, on the other hand, is the area that you do have control over. It involves the issues and events that you *can* influence in your daily life: where you go, what you do and, most importantly, your interactions with family and friends, colleagues and neighbours – the people you talk to or meet each day. You can do something about the issues, events and people in your Circle of Influence. You can be kind.

Instead of reacting to or worrying about people and events over which you have little or no control, you can focus your time and energy on things you can control. You can reach out to others and make a positive difference: you can be kind.

Think of a time you helped out another person. What did you do? Maybe you helped someone with some work they were struggling with. Perhaps you explained something to someone and made a difficult concept easier to understand. Were you able to help someone in need; someone in pain or distress? Perhaps you simply did someone a favour. Whatever it was, after you'd helped them, how did you feel? How did you feel about yourself, the other person and the world?

Although kindness and consideration expect no reward or recognition, being aware of and doing something to benefit someone else can make you and the person you are helping feel good. Chapter 1 of *Kindness* explains the many benefits of being kind; it explains how acts of kindness helps people feel respected, valued and worthy. It helps them to feel connected to others; to feel they're included, they belong and are appreciated. Kindness helps make people happy. In fact, kindness is contagious: experiencing, seeing or hearing about acts of kindness inspires others to do something kind themselves.

How, though, do you learn to be kind? You already are! It's innate in each and every one of us to be kind – to show care and concern, to want to help others. Kindness is in you and it's all around you. You just need to be more aware of it and use it more often. *Kindness* shows you how.

There are two parts to this book: Part 1 explains how to reach out to others and show your sympathy and empathy, your care, concern and consideration. You'll learn the importance of being welcoming to others; how to include them, be supportive and encouraging, and not just say thanks and express appreciation for what someone does for you, but to *show* appreciation.

There are limits to kindness though. Kindness isn't synonymous with weakness. You can be kind, considerate, generous and compassionate without being walked all over. Being kind is not about being a people pleaser – people pleasing is not coming from a genuine place of kindness; people pleasing is actually meeting your own need to be liked, rather than just wanting to make a positive difference.

Although there are situations and circumstances where an act of kindness on your part may mean putting yourself out, you're encouraged to do whatever feels natural and within your ability; to contribute what you're good at, not what you're no good at doing or not able to give.

Sometimes, though, the limits of your kindness may already be self-imposed. Are you only nice to people who you like, or who are like you? Do you divide people into those who are worthy of your goodwill and those who are not?

It's not always easy to be kind to others; when you disagree or disapprove of how someone is living their life; when they are doing or not doing something in the same way you would. Chapter 4 explains the need to respect the choices, abilities, and limits of others; to replace your assumptions and judgments with acceptance, patience and tact.

Being tactful – knowing what's appropriate to say or do to avoid giving offence – is also a useful skill for dealing with difficult or delicate situations. Whether it's letting someone down and disappointing them or giving bad news, Chapter 4 explains how you can do this with tact and kindness.

Being kind to people when you have bad news is difficult enough. But the biggest kindness challenge is when others are behaving badly towards you: when they're rude; being disrespectful or belittling, irritating or deliberately annoying. If only there were a way to make all those rude, horrible people go and live on an island together so you didn't have to deal with them! But there isn't. Chapter 5 explains how to avoid meeting rudeness with rudeness – how to avoid being unkind when others are thoughtless and inconsiderate or just downright deliberately rude. You'll read about how to be assertive, not unkind, when other people are out of order. Kindness can turn a negative situation into a positive one; if you can show a kindness to someone even though they're being unreasonable, it can make you both feel better.

In fact, being kind to others encourages you to be kind to yourself! Part 2 of *Kindness* explains how. It starts by looking at ways to feel good about yourself. You're encouraged to identify, acknowledge and appreciate your strengths, your efforts, achievements and the blessings in your life.

Reflecting on what you do well and the good things in your life is self-kindness; it's uplifting. How often, though, do you give yourself a hard time when you make a mistake, when you screw up or when you're finding it difficult to cope? Berating and blaming yourself, having

7

regrets and feeling guilty isn't exactly uplifting; it doesn't provide you with what you need most: kindness, hope and encouragement.

You wouldn't berate a friend when they made a mistake. You wouldn't be that unkind. So why be so unkind to yourself? Chapter 7 explains how, when things are difficult, you can treat yourself with the same kindness, respect and support you would give a good friend that you care about.

The last chapter – Chapter 8 – discusses the importance of self-kindness, self-care and self-compassion when you're going through a really tough time; when you've suffered a loss, a major change in your life, you're ill or injured. It's times like these that you need comfort and reassurance, kindness and compassion, not just from other people but from yourself, too.

Being kind to yourself and being kind to others, though it won't undo all the sadness and mitigate the horrors, can help lessen their force or intensity. Kindness absolutely does help make a positive difference. If only for a moment, or a few minutes, kindness counts. With kindness comes hope. Hope that things will improve; that the world *can* be a better place.

PART 1

Being Kind to Others

1
Being Kind

I've learned that people will forget what you said, people will forget what you did, but people will never forget how you made them feel.

Maya Angelou

You have the power to make the world a nicer place!

Being kind – being aware of, and doing something nice to benefit, someone else – can make both you and the person you are helping feel good.

Of course, holding a door open for someone or waiting your turn in a queue is being nice. In fact, just like saying please and thank you when you request or receive something, or saying 'excuse me' to get attention, holding the door open or waiting your turn in a queue is just plain good manners. So is asking people about their lives and interests, not just talking about your own.

As small children, we're taught good manners – we're told to say please and thank you, not to interrupt someone when they're talking, to share our things and to apologise if we do something wrong. We're constantly reminded to be polite and courteous.

What makes for good manners varies from culture to culture – in many societies it's the custom to remove your shoes before entering someone else's home. In some cultures it's considered rude or offensive to extend your left hand, rather than your right, in greeting. And if you're invited into someone's home, it's impolite to come without a gift. But wherever in the world you are, good manners are simply showing basic social skills and consideration.

So how is kindness any different? Kindness happens when you make a situation easier or less difficult for someone. Kindness involves selfless acts that either assist or lift the spirits of someone else. Kindness, like good manners and consideration, comes from a position of goodwill – wanting to do good, to do the right, proper, honourable thing. But acts of kindness are often less automatic and less formal than good manners. Kindness *can* be planned and thought out in advance, but often kind acts are spontaneous.

There need be no reason to be kind other than to make someone else smile, or be happier, but acts of kindness can also enable others to feel respected and included; to feel that they are connected to others, that they belong and are appreciated.

Whoever we are, whatever our position in life, the one concern we all have in common is how we behave towards others. We can relate to others from, for example, positions of indifference, greed, jealousy or hatred. Or we can relate to others with kindness, consideration and compassion.

What gets in the way of being kind?

Are you aware of how you relate to others throughout the day? Is it with kindness? Every day, there's potential for kindness in pretty much every encounter and interaction with other people. Often, though, we hurry through our day so focused on what we've got to do that the opportunities to interact kindly with others – with an assistant in the shop or cafe, the receptionist at the front office, an irritating family member or troubled colleague – are often forgotten or even deliberately ignored. We're just too self-involved.

Of course, you probably don't find it easy to be kind when you're wound up, tired or stressed. It's not just you though. We *all* find it difficult to think in kind, helpful ways when we feel stressed and overwhelmed. In all of us, the part of the brain (the amygdala) that's triggered when strong emotions arise – when we feel wronged in some way or when we feel stressed and agitated – is different from the part of the brain (the neo-cortex) that operates in rational and reasonable ways and enables us to remain calm, thoughtful and considerate.

When we feel emotions such as anger or guilt, when we're stressed or upset, it's not easy to be kind and considerate because the amygdala has taken over. Our ability to think in a clear, calm, rational way has been switched off.

When this happens, it's not easy to notice that someone might be in need of kindness. It's not easy, but it's not impossible. In fact, on occasions like these – when you're angry, stressed or upset – forcing yourself to do a small act of kindness can actually be the catalyst that precipitates a change in how you're feeling.

But it's not just being stressed or too busy that gets in the way of being kind. There are other reasons. Perhaps you hesitated to reach out with an act of kindness because you didn't think it would make much of a difference to the other person.

Or perhaps you weren't sure how the other person would take it; you were worried you'd say or do the wrong thing. You knew they'd had some bad news but you didn't want to say the wrong thing. You didn't want to upset them further, so you said nothing. Maybe you had an opportunity to be kind, but you thought the other person might think you were being patronising – you didn't want to risk offending them. Maybe, for example, there was an occasion when your offer to help someone carry something resulted in the other person snapping, 'I can do it myself. I don't need your help thank you very much.' So the next time you saw someone struggling to carry something, you looked the other way.

Perhaps, though, you just don't want to get too involved. If, for example, you were to offer a colleague a lift home from work one day, that might set a precedent; the other person might expect you to do it regularly. How will you get out of that? Wouldn't it be better just not to offer in the first place?

Yes, there are often difficulties and challenges to being kind, but you can take a positive approach; believe and expect that you *can* often do something kind, that you can make a difference, you can see the best in others and give others the benefit of the doubt. Even if you think a kind act won't matter or make that much difference, even if others reject your kindness, *you* know you did the right thing.

Kindness often requires courage. And courage is a strength. You can be kind *and* strong. Kindness has power and potency.

But maybe you think that by being kind you'll be susceptible to being hurt or taken advantage of. Isn't kindness all give and no take? Sure, in many situations, you take the risk of being had; there will always be someone who will try and take advantage of your kindness and generosity. But being kind is not being a doormat, it's not people pleasing. It doesn't mean *always* helping out either. It means doing what you can, when you can. It's not about duty or obligation. (That's a whole other issue!)

Kindness isn't about being responsible for other people's happiness. Kindness is about recognising that you can make a contribution – play a part – but not have to be completely responsible.

Limits of kindness

Having limits to your kindness protects you from being overly caught up in other people's feelings and situations. Limits help you to avoid constantly dropping what you're doing or what you need in order to accommodate someone else's wants and needs. Establishing and maintaining limits is not about turning your kindness off – you can still understand and identify with someone else's situation and associated feelings – you just don't have to feel obliged and totally responsible, that you *have* to do something kind to help.

There's a difference between being kind and being a people pleaser. People pleasers look for approval and validation from others; they involve themselves in other people's situations to improve their own self-worth. People pleasers are submissive and enable others to take advantage of their eagerness to please.

There's also a difference between being kind and being a rescuer: taking over and saving others from their situation. Rescuers just *have* to step in; they need to be needed. Rescuers turn other people into victims.

Kindness is not about constantly putting other people's needs before yours. It's simply about considering and connecting with others; being aware of when you could make a situation easier or less difficult for someone, make them smile and lift their spirits, help them feel that they belong and are appreciated.

Benefits of kindness

There's no doubt, though, that doing something for someone else does make you feel good. Make someone smile and you'll feel better for having done so.

A study conducted by a University of Pennsylvania research team, headed by Dr Martin Seligman, looked at the effects of writing a thank you letter and personally delivering it to someone who had never been properly thanked for their kindness. In other words, performing an act of kindness and gratitude towards someone who had themselves been kind. Participants who did this were able immediately to experience an increase in happiness scores, with benefits lasting for a month after.

Being kind takes you out of yourself; it opens you up to others and broadens your perspective. In order to be kind, you have to make an effort and be aware of what's happening around you; to be aware of what's happening for other people.

Kind gestures free you from focusing on yourself and enable you to reach out to someone else.

As the author Daniel Goleman says in his book *Social Intelligence: The New Science of Human Relationships*,

'When we focus on ourselves, our world contracts as our problems and preoccupations loom large. But when we focus on others, our world expands. Our own problems drift to the periphery of the mind and so seem smaller, and we increase our capacity for connection – or compassionate action.'

Kindness is attractive; it makes people want to be around you. They appreciate what you've done, so they want to spend more time with you.

Kindness helps people feel respected, valued and worthy. It helps them to feel connected to others; that they belong. When you're kind to people, it makes them happy. The more people who experience kindness from you, the more happy people you'll have in your life. When those around you are happier, your world becomes a brighter, better place to live.

Kindness can be persuasive and influential; it can turn a negative situation into a positive one. Even if the other person is not nice, you can be. If you can show a kindness to someone even though they're being rude or unreasonable, it can make you both feel better.

Kindness is contagious. When you're kind to others, the impact of your action doesn't necessarily stop there. Often, the recipient of your kindness, and others who see or hear about it, are inspired to do something kind themselves. Kindness elevates all who come into contact with it. When we're elevated, our spirits are lifted. As Thomas Jefferson noted, 'When any original act of charity or of gratitude, for instance, is presented either to our sight or imagination, we are deeply impressed with its beauty and feel a strong desire in ourselves of doing charitable and grateful acts also.'

Kindness is calm and peaceful. Remember a time when you were kind to someone else and think about how you felt. Was it peace and calm; a state of mutual harmony between you and the person you were kind to?

And finally, being kind to others encourages you to be kind to yourself! To see yourself as a person of worth; doing the best you can with what you have.

Aspects of kindness

So how do we become kinder? It helps to think of kindness as having several attributes and qualities that are both innate and can be developed.

Those attributes include:

Empathy: a willingness to understand other people's circumstances and feelings.
Respect: knowing that both you and other people have value and worth.
Mindfulness: being aware of what's happening around you and for other people, right here, right now.
Acceptance: recognising that what's already happened can't be changed (but what happens next can be!).
Patience: accepting that things happen in their own time.

Generosity: going out of your way: giving more than might be expected.

Positive thinking: seeing the best in other people and in yourself.

Courage: reaching out despite any apprehension you might feel.

These aspects and qualities of kindness all make the world a better place; both other people's worlds and your world too!

In a nutshell

- We can relate to others from positions of indifference, greed, jealousy or hatred. Or we can relate to others with kindness, consideration and compassion.
- Kindness comes from a position of goodwill. It's when you make a situation easier for someone, assist or lift their spirits.
- When you're stressed and overwhelmed, when you think it won't make much of a difference to the other person, it's not easy to be kind. When you feel you might say or do the wrong thing, or you just don't want to get too involved or have your kindness taken advantage of, it's not easy to be kind. It's not easy, but it's not impossible.
- There are limits, though. Establishing and maintaining limits is not about turning your kindness off – it's knowing that you don't have to feel obliged and totally responsible; that you don't *have* to do something kind to help.

- There are so many good reasons to be kind. Being kind takes you out of yourself; it opens you up to others and broadens your perspective; it allows you to be aware of what's happening around you, and to be aware of what's happening for other people.
- Kindness helps people feel respected, valued and worthy. It helps them to feel connected to others; to feel that they're included, they belong and are appreciated. It makes them happy.
- Kindness can turn a negative situation into a positive one. If you can show a kindness to someone even though they're being unreasonable, it can make you both feel better.
- Kindness is contagious. Experiencing, seeing or hearing about acts of kindness inspires others to do something kind themselves. Kindness elevates all who come into contact with it. Kindness is attractive; it makes people want to be around you.
- Being kind to others encourages you to be kind to yourself!
- Kindness is comprised of a number of qualities that are both innate and can be developed.

2
Kindness and Empathy

B eing kind – being aware of others and doing something positive for someone – may well be a choice, but the ability and the tendency to be kind is something that we all have from a very early age. You may have noticed that children begin to help others when they're very young. Without being asked, a child will often, for example, fetch something they think you might need or help a younger child to reach something. Or you may have noticed a young child show concern and compassion for a person or animal – real or fictitious – who is hurt or upset. Recently, I saw a 4-year-old comfort another child with the words 'Don't cry, no need to be sad. Would you like to play with me? Shall I give you a hug?'

Of course, as they grow older, children's desire to help and cooperate, to care and show concern becomes shaped by their interactions with others. Their interactions with family, friends, teachers and so on may either encourage or discourage them to show care and concern, to cooperate and help.

Kindness and concern, care and compassion are, then, a combination of innate and learned behaviour. When we are being kind, we are being true to our human nature.

Empathy

Kindness, like consideration and compassion, is a trait rooted in empathy. Empathy – a German word translated in 1909 by the psychologist Edward Titchener from the German *Einfühlung*: 'into feeling' – is our natural ability to see things from someone else's perspective. Empathy involves, if not understanding, at least *trying* to understand how and what someone else – a real person, a fictional character or an animal – might be experiencing, thinking or feeling.

Empathy is different from pity and sympathy. Pity is simply feeling sad and sorry for the other person. Certainly, you might do something kind out of pity for someone, but pity often treats the other person as a victim and, despite your best intentions, if you say or do something kind for someone out of pity, the other person may feel patronised and belittled.

Like pity, sympathy also involves feeling sad for someone. And as with pity, you might say or do something kind for someone out of sympathy for them. But with sympathy there is a harmony and agreement; you're not looking down on the other person. Quite the opposite: with sympathy, you understand and agree with how you think the other person is feeling about a situation.

Compassion is a step further on from sympathy. Compassion is a strong feeling of sympathy and sorrow for someone else; someone who is struck by misfortune. Along with the strong feelings of sadness and sympathy, when you feel compassion, you feel *compelled* to do something; to do something to help alleviate the other persons suffering.

Pity, sympathy and compassion are automatic reactions to someone going through a difficult time. Hearing a colleague get yelled at by your boss can immediately make you feel pity and/or sympathy for that person. You don't think about it, you just instinctively feel it.

The most immediate form of empathy is also automatic: it's when you directly feel the same emotion – distress or amusement – as someone else. When, for example, you're as frightened as the character in a scary film; as disappointed or elated as all the other fans about your team's result.

Another way you'll have experienced automatic empathy is when, for example, you wince at the same time as you see someone stub their toe, bang their head or spill a hot drink on themselves. You 'feel' their pain. Or when someone's amused reaction amuses you. A well-known YouTube video (www.youtube.com/watch?v= IIPcZJ8beME) is a good example of this. A man on a train is watching something amusing on his iPad. He laughs out loud several times and, in less than a minute, everyone else is laughing too – even though they have no idea what he's laughing about.

Another form of empathy is 'concerned empathy'. Concerned empathy is about caring and connecting, relating and engaging with someone who is suffering or in some way troubled.

Concerned empathy is more considered and deliberate than the automatic types of empathy described above. With concerned empathy, you recognise that you need to make an effort to understand; you have to work at making sense and meaning from what the other person is feeling or experiencing. You also recognise a person's feelings as valid and of worth – even if you don't agree or feel the same way about a situation.

Concerned empathy involves drawing on your own experiences and feelings to give you an insight into how the other person might be feeling. Say, for example, a friend tells you they're anxious about going to a party. Unlike your friend, the thought of going to a party where you don't know anyone is not a big deal for you. But if you can just stop for a minute and think of a different situation that makes you anxious – maybe giving a presentation to a room full of strangers – then you're more likely to be able to relate to how they're feeling: to empathise with them.

Imagine if you were, for example, asked to empathise with someone who had more money than they knew what to do with. And then they lost all that money. You might think you've nothing in common; that it'd be impossible to empathise and respond kindly. But you have lost something before, haven't you? How did you feel about that?

In another example, imagine that someone gets very irritated because the dishwasher isn't loaded the 'right' way. Or they're very upset with you because you forgot to do something you said you would. Maybe you don't think it's that important; you think they're over reacting. But with empathy you'd be aware of the fact that there are occasions when you get wound up about things that don't seem very important to others.

Develop your empathy

You can develop your ability to empathise – to 'feel with' someone else. From the list below, think of two things that you find difficult to do.

- Going to a party where you only know one or two people.
- Making a speech or giving a presentation.
- Making a journey by car, train or bus to somewhere you've not been before.
- Flying in a plane.
- Starting a new job.
- Complaining about your meal in a restaurant.
- Asking someone to turn down their iPod on a bus or train.

Although you might not be bothered about flying in a plane, maybe you do get anxious about going to a party, particularly if you don't know anyone there. You can, therefore, empathise with the person who does get anxious about flying in a plane because you know what it's like to feel anxious when you go to a party. Don't you?

It's not just everyday difficulties that you can try and empathise with. From the following list, think of two very difficult situations you've experienced:

- Bereavement.
- Physical health problems.
- Mental health difficulties.
- Accident or injury.
- Fertility problems.
- Miscarriage.
- Relationship break-up.
- Being bullied.
- Your child being bullied.
- Divorce.
- A friend or colleague seriously letting you down.
- Serious financial problems.
- Losing your job.

Now think of two situations from the list that you have not experienced.

What might the problems you've experienced have in common with those that you haven't? What emotions and feelings *might* be the same? Feelings of disappointment, despair, anxiety, anger and fear? Shame or guilt? Loneliness; feeling disconnected, left out or alone?

Maybe, although you haven't experienced being bullied, you have experienced a relationship break-up. What feelings could both those experiences have in common?

The more you are able to recall your own experience of feeling whatever the other person *could* be feeling – uncertainty and confusion, for example, or guilt, despair or anger – the better your insight, understanding and acceptance of how the other person may be feeling; the better your ability to empathise.

Challenges to empathy

With concerned empathy, you draw on your own understanding and experience to help relate to, and understand, what others feel or need. But you do have to keep in mind that others might feel or think differently from how you think they might be feeling. And actually, you might not understand at all. You just need to know that they do feel like they do and that's valid.

As the author Poorna Bell has written: 'I still haven't made peace with the fact that I may not have kids, so a toddler's birthday party is my idea of a nightmare. I don't expect others to get it, but then again I don't need their understanding – I simply need to be OK with it within myself.'

So, if you had a friend in Poorna's position, *that* might be what you need to empathise with; the fact that they're coming to terms with something.

It could be, though, that you *have* experienced the same situation that someone else is going through. But whether it's that you too may be unable to have children, or you *have* been to a party where you didn't know anyone else, or you *did* once lose your job – you can't assume you know what the other person is feeling. Maybe, for example, the person who's lost their job is not, as you might assume, upset. It could be that they're relieved!

Certainly, you should draw on your own understanding of an experience or situation and on your feelings to help relate to what someone else might be feeling. But you do need to keep in mind that the other person might feel or think differently than you do in any given situation.

The bottom line with empathy is getting that you might not get it. You don't need to have experienced the same situation as someone else, you don't have to agree with how they react to a situation to realise that, to a greater or lesser extent, they're having a hard time.

You don't have to agree that you'd feel the same way in the same situation, you just need to recognise the possible feelings and emotions. Empathy is being able to see things from the point of view of someone whose views and beliefs, likes or dislikes are different to your own.

You simply need to notice, imagine what it might be like for them and respond accordingly; with kindness and charity. Yes, charity: a kindly perspective, interpretation and understanding of a person's difficulties and challenges.

Limits to empathy

But whether or not you assume you know how the other person feels, whether it's a friend going through a relationship break-up, a colleague who is upset about a row with their boss or your partner freaking out because they've lost their phone, being empathic doesn't mean that you make the other person's situation your own.

Most of us think of health workers – paramedics, doctors, nurses – and counsellors as having concerned empathy and kindness. They do not, though, immerse themselves in the pain and difficulties of others. To do so would make them less effective at helping others. Nobody wants a therapist who gets anxious when you're anxious!

As the essayist Leslie Jamison put it, when describing a doctor who treated her, 'his calmness made me feel secure; he provided the opposite of my fear, not its echo'.

We're better at being kind and supporting others if we don't suffer along with them. Imagine, for example, a friend or colleague who's panicking because they think they're going to miss a work or study deadline. Yes, you might empathise, but it's hardly kind or helpful to panic along with them!

In difficult situations, kindness, compassion and empathy mean relating to the other person with calmness and support.

Do something

Whether it's pity, sympathy, compassion or empathy you feel, often a person's plight can leave you feeling that there's nothing you can do. And so you do nothing. But one simple act can make a difference. Sometimes the most simple kindness you can give another human being is to acknowledge them.

On 19 April 1987, Princess Diana visited AIDS patients at the UK's first unit dedicated to treating people with HIV and AIDS at London's Middlesex Hospital. A famous photograph shows her shaking a patient's hand. The gesture challenged the widely held, but incorrect, belief that HIV or AIDS could be transmitted by touch.

Today it might not seem such a big deal, since we know that HIV – the virus that can lead to AIDS – can't be transmitted by a simple handshake. But things were different in the 1980s. Although researchers at the Centre for Disease Control had already concluded that the disease could not be transmitted through casual contact, most people weren't convinced. In 1985, for example, a poll conducted by the *Los Angeles Times* found that 50% of respondents favoured quarantining people with AIDS.

Diana's gesture of kindness and compassion had a huge impact for others in a way that speeches, public service announcements and TV interviews never could.

She didn't just feel compassion, sympathy and empathy, she let those emotions motivate her to *do* something; something kind. It might not have alleviated the other person's suffering, but it was a positive gesture of kindness and support.

Be a good listener

To be kind is more important than to be right. Many times what people need is not a brilliant mind that speaks but a special heart that listens.

F. Scott Fitzgerald

What, then, can you say or do when a friend or family member tells you his wife has left him? Or that their partner has been in a car accident or their child has been diagnosed with a serious heart condition? What do you say and do when a family member, a friend or colleague or your partner tells you that they're desperately unhappy and want to quit their job? Or a young person tells you they want to quit university?

When you feel like you don't know what to do or say, you just simply need to show that you care. You can't take the pain or frustration away. But you can show your care, concern and compassion. You can do this by listening to the other person. Do nothing but simply listen to what they're saying and feeling. Don't interrupt, don't try to fix it, pacify them, offer solutions or stop their experience or expression of what they're thinking or feeling. You don't need to say anything, just being willing to listen can help a person feel less alone and isolated.

Be patient. You might want to know more details about what's happened and how they feel about it, but, first, let the other person express themselves. Whatever they say, however long it takes them to tell you, or however brief, when you think they've finished, count to three before you respond. This gives the other person an opportunity to continue, but it's not so long a pause that it appears you're not going to respond.

By giving them a chance to say what's happened and what they're feeling, by trying to understand what the other person is saying and feeling, you are trying to see things from their point of view; you're being empathic.

What to say? Do's and don'ts

If the other person has simply made a brief announcement, you might need to know more. For example, someone might tell you that they're desperately unhappy in their job or on their university course. Simply ask them: 'Can you tell me more about that?' Other times, someone may have poured their heart out and given you a detailed description of their situation. In that case, you might start by clarifying and confirming what you've understood. Just say: 'So, can I just be clear, you're saying that ... have I got that right?'

Do ask about how someone feels about what's happened: 'How do you feel about that?' Even if you think you know, let them tell you.

Don't say 'I know how you feel'. Instead, say something like: 'I'm sorry that happened. It must be hard/confusing/annoying/disappointing/upsetting for you.' In this way, you're validating that whatever it is, you understand that for them, it is hard, difficult, upsetting or confusing or whatever it is they could be feeling. The other person might agree, or they might disagree and explain further. Recently, for example, I was talking with someone who told me that two years ago she'd lost all her hair as a result of chemotherapy. I assumed that being bald must've been awful for her. I was wrong. 'Not at all,' she said, 'I loved the freedom of no hair.'

Do ask open questions to encourage the other person to talk; to express their thoughts and feelings. Open questions usually begin with what, why, how, tell me, explain. For example: 'Why do you think he said that?', 'How did that happen?' Don't interrogate them though.

Don't think you can make someone talk to you. It can take time for someone to feel able to talk openly, and putting pressure on them to talk might dissuade them from saying anything at all.

Do try and stay calm. Even though someone else's distress might be upsetting, try to stay calm. This will help the other person feel calmer too, and let them feel that they can talk freely, without upsetting you.

Don't give your thoughtful analysis of what went wrong and why.

When your friend is turned down for a job or place on the course, or your sister's husband leaves her, or someone tells you they've had a terrible day at work, or had a row with their partner, parent or teenager, your perspective might be useful but don't assume that you know how they feel or what will help.

Don't tell them how to make tomorrow better. Sometimes solutions are unnecessary, so don't feel you have to provide one. You may feel powerless about not being able to offer some practical help, so don't suggest a juice fast, or that they need to meditate, or that you'll lend them that brilliant self-help book about being happier every day. Not now. Just listen. They may well appreciate you just listening more than your advice.

Don't slip into clichés. It's easy to give unhelpful platitudes that offer no comfort but just irritate the other person. Don't say things like:

- Everything happens for a reason.
- God never gives you more than you can handle.
- It was meant to be.
- It could be worse.
- What's done is done.
- Time heals all wounds.
- You'll get over it.

Do say: 'I'm sorry you're going through this.'

Do suggest a walk or a drive. Sometimes it's easier to talk things through when you're both moving. The simple action of moving forward helps a person's mind to move forward, too. If someone is struggling to find a solution to a problem – feeling stuck in their job or a relationship – a walk in the park or countryside or a drive really can help open perspective and move things forward.

Giving advice and information: do's and don'ts

Do share your experience. Being kind and considerate means looking beyond yourself and making the time and effort to think about how others might be feeling and to be aware and notice how your behaviour can make a positive impact. You make a point of looking for opportunities when you could help someone out. Sometimes, that can mean sharing your own experience.

Sharing your experiences and feelings with someone creates mutual understanding and empathy. The best support groups do this. Rather than being pity fests, where everyone wallows in their shared difficulties, a good support group is more constructive; it helps people to feel less alone, provides ideas and information, enabling the other person to identify their options, make a decision, move forward and take control.

If you've had a similar experience or know of someone else who has, just say: 'That's happened to me/happened to my friend. Let me know if you think it would be helpful for you to hear about it.' The other person's thoughts and feelings about their situation might be different to yours, but by sharing your own experience, they might pick up some insights rather than feeling they'd been *told* what to do.

Do be positive. Think back to the last time you gave advice to someone. Did you express concern and understanding, or were you frustrated, angry or worried about their situation? When you feel like this, you may think you are giving good advice but you're probably coming across as negative or critical. You're certainly not coming across with kindness. Rather than starting your advice with, 'Why didn't you … ?' or 'You should have … ', accept what's done is done, and focus on what they can do next. Ask: 'Do you want some ideas to improve the situation?' Or 'Can I suggest something?' Or 'Can I give you my opinion/advice?' And say something like 'How about … ?' or 'It might help to consider … '.

Do know when to let go. Even if the other person asks for your advice, they won't necessarily take it. You can never be sure that your advice is really right for them.

Don't be surprised if a person rejects your good advice and decides to follow their own course of action.

Do keep your advice short and to the point. Even if there appears to be a right solution, think what possible courses of action there might be and, together with the other person, consider the pros and cons of each. Help them to come to their own conclusions and decisions. Whenever you've talked for a few minutes, bring it back to them. 'What are your thoughts about that?'

Do know that there are no magic words that will make everything okay. The best you can do is listen, follow your heart, be open to emotions, validate feelings and support them in the ways you believe are best.

What to do? Do's and don'ts

When you're aware that someone is struggling or suffering in some way, be empathetic. Remember when someone has shown *you* kindness and compassion. What did they do that helped? What wasn't so helpful?

Do know that small gestures make a big difference.

Do keep in touch; a text message or email just to let them know that you're thinking of them can make a difference to how someone feels. It's difficult to know what to say to someone who is going through a tough time, so often we choose to say nothing. But even if you don't have all the right words, let someone know you're thinking of them. Say something like: 'I'm sorry to hear about what happened. I wanted to call and tell you that I'm thinking of you.'

Don't just ask 'How are you?' Instead, be more specific. Ask: 'How have you been today/this week/the last few weeks?'

Don't hang up if they don't answer the phone. Do leave a message. It's not a problem if they don't return the call. They may not feel up to talking, so simply express your thoughts and well wishes in a voicemail message.

Do send a card.

Don't think an email or text is inappropriate. Do send a text of a few words, and a bunch of flowers emoji or whatever is appropriate. You don't always need to talk about their situation, you're simply connecting; letting the other person know you're thinking about them. So, if you're hesitating to send a text saying hi or you have something else to share – an amusing story – know that virtual connecting is valid: it's kind and supportive. It's better than doing nothing.

Don't say: 'If you need anything, let me know.' Why not? Because everyone says that. It puts the onus on the other person to think of what they need, who and when to ask.

Don't just ask 'How can I help?' or 'What can I do?' either. The person might be at a loss to answer. It's better to ask 'Would it help if I … ' or say 'I would like to … '. Make some suggestions, offer to do something specific. Say: 'I was thinking, I could bring you lunch/drop off take-away/go to the shops/clean the house/have the children for the afternoon/walk the dog/give you a lift to … Would that be okay, or is there something else I can help with?'

Do think practically and bring necessities that your friend and/or their family may need during a difficult or challenging time. You might ask 'I'm going to the super-market – anything I can pick up for you while I'm there?'

Do know that you may need to make the first move; to help without being asked, even if you're not sure you'll be doing the right thing.

Do bring treats. If you know a certain thing will bring a smile to their face – their favourite ice-cream, M&S

sandwich or ready meal, flowers from your garden, strawberries or chocolate – then take it or send it over.

Do offer to do something normal – go to a show, a film, an exhibition or a sports match. Or go for a walk – either chatting about other parts of both your lives or walking in companionable silence. Maybe they don't want to talk so, instead, do something nice together; cook a meal together. Play cards, a board game or a computer game. You might offer to come over and watch something on TV and bring a take-away to eat together; sit and read or do some work on your laptop while the person is in bed.

He took me out in his car on Sundays ... and sometimes just sat watching telly with me and saying little ... It's hard to explain how much that comforted me, like a glimpse of normality in my topsy-turvy new world of illness ... And the almost daily calls from my oldest son, full of love and kindness, have comforted and restored me more than I can ever say.

Guardian journalist Ruth Pitt, recovering
from a severe attack of Crohn's disease

Do learn about the other person's situation to help you think about other ways you could support them.

If, for example, a friend has been diagnosed with a mental health problem, MIND's website (See 'Useful Websites' at the back of this book) provides information about different types of mental health problems, including pages on what friends and family can do to help in each case.

Do help the other person to identify things they can try to do themselves.

Do support them to get information and/or help. Suppose, for example, a friend had a health problem – physical or mental health. You could help to write down the questions that they want to ask the doctor.

You might go to appointments with them if they want you to; just being there in the waiting room can help someone feel reassured.

Don't think that you can force someone to get help (if they're over 18 and are not posing immediate danger to themselves or someone else). If you feel that someone is clearly struggling but can't or won't reach out for help, and won't accept any help you offer, it's understandable to feel frustrated and distressed. But you won't always know the full story, and there may be reasons they don't want to tell you about. Just let them know you care about them and you'll be there if they change their mind.

Don't be an overbearing do-gooder. There's a difference between being kind and supportive and taking over. Ask yourself: Do I feel like I just have to step in? Or is it something they can do and work out for themselves? Trust and respect other people to identify how they want to handle things. You can still be involved, just be aware of getting too involved.

Do set limits. Remember you have limits to your kindness and helping abilities. Whatever someone else's emotional problems or difficulties – whether it's a friend's bereavement, a friend going through a disciplinary procedure at work or it's simply your partner losing their keys – do avoid becoming overly involved.

It doesn't mean turning your kindness, concern and empathy off; you can still try to understand how someone else feels – you just don't have to feel responsible or that you have to undertake some sort of emotional or practical rescue, freeing them from their experience and feelings.

Do what you're good at; don't do what you're no good at

Of course, the do's and don'ts described here don't all apply to every difficult situation and circumstance someone is going through. Some of the do's and don'ts are appropriate for some situations. Other do's and don'ts are appropriate for other situations.

Not only that, but it's important to know that no one is good at every one of the 'do's'. Go with your strengths. Only offer what you're good at. If it's mundane chores – shopping and cleaning and walking their dog – then offer to do mundane chores. If you're good at listening, then meet up or phone them and listen. If you're uncomfortable listening to someone talk about their situation, but you have no problem sitting watching TV or making a meal together, then do that. If you're good at finding appropriate little gifts or YouTube videos that could bring a smile to the person's face, then do just that.

The more you show a kindness that reflects who you are, the more you'll feel good about showing that kindness and the more likely you'll be to offer it again. Don't offer to do something you're no good at and then feel resentful or negative in some other way about doing it. Offer what kindness you can and feel good about it.

Trust yourself to do the right thing. Know that your values, concern and small gestures do make a big difference.

In a nutshell

- Kindness – an ability and tendency that we all have from when we're very young – is a combination of innate and learned behaviour. When we're being kind, we are being true to our human nature.
- Empathy involves, if not understanding, at least *trying* to understand, how and what someone else – a real person, a fictional character or an animal – might be experiencing, thinking or feeling.
- Like pity, sympathy and compassion, empathy can be an instinctive, automatic reaction to someone going through a difficult time.
- Concerned empathy is more considered and deliberate. You need to make an effort to understand what the other person is feeling or experiencing. You recognise a person's feelings as valid and of worth – even if you don't agree or feel the same way about a situation. You might not feel, for example,

anxious in a particular situation, but you have felt anxious in another situation, so you can empathise with how they're feeling.

- The bottom line with empathy is getting that you might not get it. You don't need to have experienced the same situation as someone else, you don't have to agree with how they react to a situation to realise that, to a greater or lesser extent, they're having a hard time.
- Being empathic doesn't mean that you make the other person's situation your own. We're better at being kind and supporting others if we don't suffer along with them.
- You can't take the pain or frustration away. But you can show your care, concern and compassion.
- One simple act can make a difference. Sometimes the simplest kindness you can give another human being is to acknowledge them.
- Listen. Don't interrupt, pacify or offer solutions. Listen and try to understand what the other person is saying and feeling. Try to see things from their point of view. If you can do this, you're being empathic.
- Don't say 'I know how you feel'. Don't give your thoughtful analysis of what went wrong and why and how to make tomorrow better. Instead, say something like: 'I'm sorry that happened. It must be hard/confusing/annoying/disappointing/upsetting for you.' Do ask questions, but don't interrogate.
- Do know that small gestures make a big difference. Do keep in touch: an email, text, a call, a card. Do bring treats. Do offer to do something normal.

- You may need to make the first move; to help without being asked, even if you're not sure you'll be doing the right thing. Do ask, 'Would it help if I ... ' or say, 'I would like to ... Would this be okay, or is there something else I can help with?'
- Do support the other person to identify things they can try to do themselves. Support them to get information and/or help.
- Share your experiences. Just say 'That's happened to me/happened to my friend. Let me know if you think it would be helpful for you to hear about it.' The other person's thoughts and feelings about their situation might be different to yours, but by sharing your own experience, they might pick up some insights rather than feel they've been *told* what to do.
- Don't be an overbearing do-gooder. There's a difference between being kind and supportive and taking over. Do set limits. Remember you have limits to your helping abilities. Avoid becoming overly involved.
- Don't think you can make someone talk to you. Don't think that you can force someone to get help. The best you can do is listen, follow your heart, be open to emotions, validate feelings and support them in the ways you believe are best.
- The more you show a kindness that reflects who you are and what you're good at, the more you'll feel good about showing that kindness and the more likely you'll be to offer it again. Trust yourself to do the right thing. Offer what kindness you can and feel good about it.

3
Go Out of Your Way to Make a Difference

Be welcoming, approachable and inclusive

Imagine that you are invited to a party. Your friend greets you when you arrive, but for the rest of the evening they're darting about looking stressed. They leave you to get your own drink and don't introduce you to anyone. You try joining in a couple of conversations with people, but no one seems that interested in chatting to you.

Do you feel welcome? It's unlikely! You can probably think of other times and situations where you've not felt welcome; ignored and excluded.

On the other hand, you can probably remember times when someone made a point of welcoming and including you – as a new employee, at someone else's family occasion, a meeting or conference, as a parent of young children at a toddler club, maybe on holiday at a local community's celebration?

Whether it's welcoming friends and acquaintances into your home, customers, clients or visitors to your workplace or a new member to a club you belong to, it's important to treat people with kindness and respect; to make them feel welcome – that you're pleased they're there.

The obvious place to start making someone feel welcome is when they arrive. Of course, you don't want to embarrass them by making a fuss – you simply need to stop what you're doing, smile, say hello and shake their hand or, if it's appropriate, give them a kiss and/or a hug. If you've never met them before, introduce yourself.

But being welcoming is more than just saying hello to someone and saying you're pleased to see them or meet them. It's also about making them feel included and that they belong. Aim to be inclusive: enable people to feel part of something; to feel that they can be involved in what you're doing or talking about.

If you're at a party or work event, introduce them to other people – people they may have something in common with. For example, you might introduce your sister to a colleague by saying 'Ali, Josh has just come back from a trip to Italy. Josh, Ali lived in Italy for a couple of years.'

If you can't think of something they've got in common, tell one person something interesting about the other person. For example, 'Theresa, Boris has just been telling me all about his interest in cycling. He's cycled all over London; he knows London like the back of his hand.'

Considerate people introduce other people who don't know each other and make a point of including people in a conversation so no one is left out. So, if someone isn't saying much in a group, ask them a specific question to bring them in. Don't draw attention to it by saying something like 'You're awfully quiet, Rosa', just say 'Rosa, what do you think about what we were just saying … ?'

As well as making a point of including others, do be aware that when, for example, you're at a pub or club, at a party, meeting or a networking event, you may inadvertently be excluding others from joining you. It's easy to circle up in a group of four or five of you, or pair off with one other person. But large groups or pairs of people tend to be less approachable for others. Joining a group of five or six people is scary, as is approaching two people who are involved in a conversation. A group of three people is easier; it makes you more approachable for others.

What to say

Be open to small talk. Maybe you think small talk is shallow or boring, that it feels fake and a waste of time and that there's more to life than talking about the weather or the price of fish. Get over yourself!

There's nothing 'small' about small talk. With small talk, it's not what you talk about – it's simply about connecting: coming across as an approachable, friendly person who is open to exchanging a few pleasantries. You don't have to impress, you don't have to be brilliant. You just have to be nice. Smile, ask questions, take a genuine interest in the other person and say something about yourself.

It doesn't matter if you make the usual comments: 'It's so cold today!' Or questions: 'How do you know Martine?', 'Have you been here before?', 'What do you do?'. But you do need to be interested in, and follow up on, their answers.

Comment or ask their opinion on something that both you and the other person are experiencing; where you're both at and what's around you. For example, say 'I really love this restaurant'. It's likely they'll ask you why, which opens up another opportunity for conversation. And if they don't, ask what they think of the place.

If you're still feeling apprehensive, imagine that the other person is already your friend – as you know a friend would respond positively if you approached them.

Maybe you heard something interesting on the news. Tell them and then ask their opinion about it. Is there an app you can't live without? Did you lose your keys or find £10? Tell the other person, then ask if they've ever done the same. Don't worry about having the 'right' things to say. You could say something about a book you're reading, a blog or website you've found interesting. What about a film, TV show or box set you've recently watched? Tell the other person and ask if they've read, watched or read something good recently.

Here are some ideas for questions you can ask to start a conversation or keep it going.

Work
- What was your first ever job?
- What was the best or worst job you've ever had? Why?
- If you weren't working here, where would you like to be working? Why?
- Would you rather work four 10-hour days or five 8-hour days? Why?
- When you were a child, what did you think you were going to do when you grew up – was it this job?

Entertainment
- If you could only watch one genre of movies/books for the rest of your life, what would it be? Why?
- Who are your favourite film stars/solo artists/ bands? Why? What do you like about them?

Food
- If you could only eat three things for the rest of your life, what would they be? Why?
- What's the weirdest thing you've ever eaten?
- What's your favourite comfort food? Why?

Travel
- If you could fly and stay anywhere for free, where would you go? Why?

- What's the best and worst holiday you've been on? Why?
- If you could take six months paid leave, where would you go and what would you do? Why?

Go the extra mile; be generous

Being welcoming and inclusive is a basic human kindness. But by making an extra effort – going out of your way to be welcoming, approachable and inclusive – you're not just being kind and considerate, you're being generous. Generosity, like kindness, involves doing or giving something willingly to make other people's lives easier and more pleasant. But generosity means giving *more* than might be expected.

You have an opportunity to be generous whenever you're aware that extra effort on your part could make all the difference. You can be generous to others with your time, your money, your possessions, with your energy and skills. You can also be generous with your knowledge and encouragement.

Be generous with your encouragement

To encourage means 'to put courage into'. When you encourage someone, you give them the courage or confidence to make a start, to try for something; a colleague to apply for a promotion, for example, or a friend to retrain or sign up to learn a new skill.

Or you might encourage someone to continue to do something – to cope with a situation despite some difficulties; keep training for the marathon or keep going with their studies or job seeking. Or maybe you'd encourage someone who's aiming to achieve something – a friend who's trying to recover from an accident or health problem, or a colleague who's aiming to get fit and healthy.

There's a range of reasons why someone might need encouraging, but where do you start? Well, you begin by acknowledging the challenges. If someone is unsure about their abilities, find out what, exactly, their feelings and concerns are. Encouraging others means you don't deny the difficulties. Instead, acknowledge them and tell them they can manage the difficulties and succeed.

Point out what qualities and strengths they have that will help them solve problems and contribute to overcoming difficulties and achieving what they're aiming for. If you can support people and encourage them when things are difficult, you're being positive and optimistic. And that's being kind.

Do empathise: whether it's making a journey, taking a test or sitting an exam, attending a medical appointment or treatment, going for a job interview or sky diving, think of the times and the ways that you've been encouraged by others to give you some ideas about how to encourage someone else. Maybe someone simply showed an interest in what you were doing. Do the same for someone else. It's encouraging for them to know that someone is genuinely interested in what they're trying to achieve.

Remind them of their reason to achieve something; what they'll gain. Maybe it's a financial or material gain. Perhaps they'll improve themselves or their situation in some way. Whatever it is, tell them and remind them of it.

Get the other person to visualise what success will look and feel like. Encourage them to feel and see what's possible; a clear picture of what they're aiming for. Sometimes, though, what someone is trying to cope with or achieve seems so big that it feels overwhelming for them. Encourage them to identify what they can do and to take it one step at a time.

Don't, though, wait until they've succeeded or achieved their goal to say something positive. Acknowledge their efforts and point out what they've already achieved – that they've done so well already with, for example, their studies, caring for their partner or a parent. When you see someone making progress, say something; give a compliment or praise. If an encouraging thought comes to mind, share it! It may not have the same effect if you wait. Don't hold back. Tell them face to face, by text or email. People rarely get personal mail anymore, so write and post a card with a note of encouragement.

Kind words can be short and easy to speak, but their echoes are truly endless.

Mother Teresa

Support others; mentoring and advocating

As well as expressing encouragement, you can also connect with, encourage and help others by doing something. You've got a unique set of skills, knowledge and experiences. You can share and contribute your insights and perspectives, your skills and knowledge. One way you can do this is as a mentor.

Mentoring is an opportunity to use your skills and experiences to make a real difference to someone who's only just starting out and is less experienced than you. You can share the knowledge, the lessons, experiences and skills you've accumulated.

Formal mentoring usually happens in the workplace; it's structured and monitored. If an organisation has a mentoring scheme, it will have experienced members of staff to support and inform new members of staff until they feel confident in their role and the culture of the organisation. Voluntary organisations also run mentoring schemes. As a mentor with, for example, The Prince's Trust, you can make a real difference to the lives of young people finishing a Prince's Trust programme, providing a young person with support to move towards employment, education or training; to identify goals and targets to work towards. (See the back of the book for 'Useful Websites'.)

Informal mentoring, though, usually happens between friends and family during life changes.

In a range of circumstances when going through a change in life – becoming a parent, retirement, divorcing, moving somewhere new, coping with illness or disability – others can benefit from the knowledge of someone who has gone through a similar experience or change; they can provide insights, advice and guidance.

If you offer to mentor someone in an informal way, a key requisite is empathy; remember what it was like when you were just starting out or feeling inexperienced in an area of your life. Crucially, though, you'll need to be sensitive to the unique needs of others. Do recognise that your circumstances and how you coped as, for example, a first-time parent may be different for someone else. Be aware, too, of when others require your direct assistance and support and when to step back and let them manage themselves.

Share your knowledge and skills

A mentor is willing to show, explain or teach someone less experienced in a particular field or subject. But they might not be struggling, they may simply have expressed an interest in something you are good at – photography, Mexican cooking, website programming, gardening. Share your skills. If someone you know has expressed an interest in what you do, offer to teach them what you know.

Advocate

Another way of encouraging and supporting someone else is as an advocate. The word 'advocacy' comes from Latin and means 'to add a voice'. Advocacy involves speaking or doing something on behalf of a person about issues that matter to them in situations where they don't feel able to speak or do something for themselves.

Advocates help a person be involved in decisions about their lives, explore choices and options, express their views and wishes, make sure their voice is heard – that others listen to their views and concerns.

This might include helping someone contact relevant people, accessing information, writing letters on someone's behalf and helping them make informed decisions. As an advocate you might also go with a person to meetings or interviews in a supportive role.

Crucially, though, advocates don't offer their opinion or advice and they certainly don't take over. They simply act as the voice or the physical ability for someone else.

You might advocate for someone else – a friend, family member or neighbour – in an informal way. But you can also advocate in a more formal way; there's a range of organisations that offer training and volunteer positions for mentoring, befriending and advocacy services.

There are people in our world who need someone to speak out for them. You don't have to take on that cause by yourself, but instead join others. It could be Amnesty International – a global movement of more than 7 million people who take injustice personally – or it could be speaking up for neighbours at a local council meeting, writing letters and making a need heard.

Speak out

While advocating involves representing another person's needs and concerns, there may be times when you feel compelled to speak out unprompted; to call someone to account or challenge a perceived wrongdoing against someone else without being asked.

Sometimes it seems like staying silent is the wiser choice. On the other hand, just one person speaking up can often be enough to encourage other dissenters to speak up too. Here's what happened to Callum:

> One day I was serving at the counter and in front of customers the manager snapped 'Callum can't you get anything right? That's not how to make a cappuccino. Surely you learnt how to do this in your training last week. What is it you're doing here?' A customer standing at the counter spoke out, 'He's right, Callum. What are you thinking, working here? You're meant for much more than this.' I really appreciated their kindness and support in the face of my public humiliation. It gave me the courage to say, 'Yes. Please don't speak to me like that – please just explain what I can do to make it better.'

When something strikes you as unfair or uncalled for, if you feel you can speak out, do so. Have courage. A firm, polite challenge is sometimes all that is needed. Make sure, though, that the other person won't suffer as a result of you speaking out on their behalf. Keep them and yourself safe; don't risk getting into a heated argument or a fight. If you can't say something there and then, maybe offer your support – some kind words – in private. The customer in the example above could, for example, have waited until the manager was out of earshot and then said something supportive to Callum.

Express your appreciation

> Feeling gratitude and not expressing it is like wrapping a present and not giving it.
>
> *William Arthur Ward*

Standing up for someone and speaking out can certainly be a challenge. What shouldn't be so difficult, though, is to express appreciation to others and explain how they've made a positive difference; to give praise and compliments.

We can all agree that you should say 'thanks' when, for example, someone holds open a door for you, gives you directions, invites you to something, does you a favour or gives you a gift. How often, though, do you thank someone for waiting for you when you're running late? If you've poured your heart out to a friend, do you thank them for listening to you when you're sad, upset or stressed and just need to talk?

Take the time to give a sincere thank you to people. For example: 'Thank you for taking the time to talk to me about this,' 'Thanks for taking the time to write/phone/call in when I was stressed/freaked out/sad/upset. Thank you for the support.'

Saying 'thank you' not only shows appreciation, it's also an acknowledgement – you've shown that you recognise that the other person gave you their time, energy or help. When you don't acknowledge – take for granted something someone's done for you – you don't recognise its true value.

Giving praise and compliments

However, you can extend your appreciation further by acknowledging the positive difference that their actions had for you. For example, 'Thank you for taking the time to talk to me about this. *Your listening really helped me think more clearly about the issue.*'

Explain what a difference their efforts have made. People feel good if they know that they made a difference. So, if what someone has done has had a positive effect on you, tell them:

'Thanks for talking with me about that. You explained it so well. Now I understand how to … '

'Thanks for going to the shops for me. You've saved me so much time.'

'Thanks for fixing that for me. You've saved me having to buy a new one and that means I've saved a lot of money! Thank you.'

Whether it's a friend who's listened to you, or a company or individual that's provided a good service, when you tell the other person that they've made a positive difference, they can then feel good about themselves and encouraged because of the impact their actions had on you.

But as well as acknowledging and expressing appreciation to someone you know who's helped you, you can also connect with people you've never met but whose actions have made a positive difference for you. Next time you read something that really encourages or motivates you, let the writer know. Make a comment on a website or blog; let them know how they helped or inspired you with their book, website or blog. Write a positive review or comment.

Compliments and praise

Of course, acknowledgements and appreciation aren't only for when someone has done something for you.

Compliments – expressions of praise and admiration – should also be extended to someone who has achieved or overcome something, has made a special effort or put extra time into something that has benefited someone else.

You don't need to worry about getting the wording just right. Genuine sentiment phrased a bit awkwardly is better than saying nothing at all. My friend Gina recently told me:

> I still remember being told I had a lovely smile from my English teacher over 35 years ago – possibly the only compliment my gawky teenage self received. It doesn't hurt and it can make someone's day. Or year!

The best way to ensure that you sound genuine is to compliment someone when the positive thought comes to you. Start with the reason why you are complimenting or praising the other person. Be specific. Sometimes the most memorable compliments are the most specific ones, because it shows that you noticed. For example:

'The way you handled that question at the meeting was perfect. You totally refocused the discussion.'
'You've done so well caring for your partner. I know it was difficult for you, but I'd just like to say well done for managing so well.'
'You handled that rude customer so well. Well done for being so patient with him.'
'I love your outfit; the scarf is beautiful; I just love how you've tied it'
'What a fab hat! And you wear it so well.'
'I love your home! The rug in the living room is beautiful – where's it from?'

Look for ways to compliment people for their actions. Acknowledge personal qualities or special efforts; a person's concern and patience or the extra time they put into something. When, for example, a colleague does a great job on a project, compliment them on a job well done. Notice what someone is wearing and how they look. Compliments (appropriate compliments) on appearance make people feel good.

Notice the work someone does. It could be someone who serves you in a shop or cafe, it could be something about someone's business or someone in your office. Make a positive comment about their work or business.

If you can't tell a person to their face, put it in writing. Your words will let the other person know that their actions have been noticed and appreciated. And putting it in writing shows even more effort on your part while also giving the person a permanent reminder of the praise.

Compliment people on things you know they value and are proud of. Praise a parent for their child. There are few compliments more gratifying than when someone praises your child. When the opportunity arises, compliment someone on the abilities or behaviour of their offspring.

Take a look around and see who you can pay a compliment to today. If you like something someone has done, has made, is wearing and so on, don't keep it to yourself. Tell them! Let the other person know that their intentions, efforts or actions have been noticed and help them feel good about themselves and their abilities.

Sometimes, a person may feel embarrassed and dismiss your compliment. Be kind, don't press the point, just repeat it once and if they dismiss it again simply smile, say 'OK' and move onto something else.

Don't just express appreciation, show it

Saying thank you, giving compliments or praise are simple acknowledgements and ways of showing appreciation of someone else's words or actions.

When you appreciate and express acknowledgement of someone or something, you recognise the value of something a person has done or given you – their contribution, their time, advice, support. But appreciation can, and often should, be more than simply acknowledging and saying thanks.

Saying thanks and expressing appreciation is simply words. But when you *show* appreciation for something, you demonstrate your feelings through actions. You reciprocate; you give in return.

Reciprocation can be direct and reflect what the other person has done for you – for example, a friend is there for you when you need to talk to someone about a problem and then when your friend needs someone to talk to, you're there for your friend.

Reciprocation can also be indirect: for example, your partner cooked, so you wash up. Or your neighbour fixed your bike, so you show your appreciation by buying them a bottle of wine.

Reciprocation is a way of showing appreciation. Of course, it's not necessary to keep a score in relationships with family, friends, neighbours or colleagues, but often reciprocating *is* necessary; it's the right thing to do. Reciprocating isn't just expressing your appreciation and gratitude, it's making an effort – going out of your way to show the other person how you feel.

Make kindness a habit

Habit is a cable; we weave a thread each day, and at last we cannot break it.

Horace Mann

It isn't necessary to be kind all your waking hours, and occasional attempts to 'notice the little things more' – to be kind, caring, empathic and compassionate – are well meaning; but distractions and preoccupations take over and resolutions to be kind can fall by the wayside.

What to do? You need to make kindness a habit; make a concerted effort to be kind on a regular basis, until it becomes 'a cable', as the educational reformer Horace Mann says in the quote above.

Establishing specific ways of thinking and doing is not difficult provided those ways are constantly repeated. How come? When you think or do something, you create connections, or 'neural pathways', in your brain. Then, every time you repeat that thought or action, every time you continue using these new pathways, they become stronger and more established.

It's like walking through a field of long grass: each step helps to create a new path and every time you walk that new path you establish a clear route which becomes easier to use each time. It becomes a habit to use that route. In the same way, it can become a habit to be kind.

But since your distracted and preoccupied mind isn't always going to remind you to be kind, you need something else to remind you. Write notes that say: Be kind. Place them on the wall above your desk, or on the fridge to remind you. Make the words 'Be kind' a screensaver on your phone.

Then, from the list below, choose a number of kind gestures and actions you could carry out over the next month.

- Divert one specific expense for a set period of time – a week, a month – to a charity or cause. You could choose to bring a lunch to work, or give up a coffee. Donate the money you save to a specific charity or cause that you feel strongly about: the environment, child welfare or animal rights, Amnesty, the Red Cross, a cancer or Parkinsons charity.

- Respond to every text and email. Even if you have to say, 'Just to let you know I got your email and I'll get back to you later/tomorrow/next week.' People like to know they're not being ignored.
- Each day, send an email specifically designed to help somebody else. Make introductions, send some encouragement, offer a helpful resource or link; a useful new piece of information. Don't keep it to yourself. Each and every day, you're likely to have something worthwhile to share that could be beneficial to your friends, family or colleagues or just someone you met at a party.
- 'Pay it forward' is an expression for describing the beneficiary of a good deed repaying it to others instead of to the original benefactor. If you receive a kindness today, let it be the prompt to do something kind for someone else.
- Cheer someone up. Find an old photo of you and a friend and get it printed and sent to them by an online photo printing company. Try www.photobox.co.uk.
- Do a chore that you don't normally do for someone else. Cook, shop, take the rubbish out, clean the loo, get the car cleaned, change the ink cartridge in the printer.
- Phone friends and family on their birthdays. Not just a message on Facebook.
- Be generous when tipping. Give an extra £1 tip, spend an extra 10 minutes with someone who needs or will appreciate it.
- Kindness doesn't have to be big, elaborate round-the-clock displays of selflessness and generosity. It

can be little things that don't take too much effort. Know that the smallest gestures can make a big difference. Never underestimate the power of good morning texts. Send a text to someone tomorrow morning saying 'Morning! How's things with you?'

- Get in touch with someone you haven't been in contact with for a while. Write them a card, email or text just to let them know you were thinking about them.
- Send a surprise gift to a friend. When you find something that's easily affordable that you know a friend would like, don't wait for a birthday or Christmas, send it now.
- Send a surprise book to someone from an online retailer.
- Be thoughtful. Did your colleague have a bad day today? Bring them a coffee tomorrow morning.
- Spread the word. If you know someone who decorates or cleans, is a plumber or a gardener, and you could recommend them, let others know.
- Invite people out. Ask someone to do something nice with you: the cinema, a show, a walk, a meal. Really, how often do you make the first move and ask a friend to do something with you? Is it always the other person that organises and invites you out?
- If you hear about an event – an exhibition, a film, a band, pub quiz, a firework display, street party, a new teashop, an 'open garden' – that you think someone you know would enjoy, invite them to it. Ask them if they'd like to go to it with you.
- Get in touch with someone you know who is going through a difficult time. Phone or write them a card,

email or text, cook a meal or send flowers or some
other thoughtful expression to let them know you
care and are thinking about them.

- Hold the door open for someone and smile at them
  as you do. In a supermarket queue, let the person
  who seems rushed go in front of you. And on the
  road, be kind to other drivers. In a queue, let people
  merge in.
- Buy someone cake or some fresh fruit – sum-
  mer strawberries or raspberries. It could be your
  colleagues, neighbours, family or friends. Surprise
  them.
- Offer to help deliver or collect something for someone.
- Save a life. Donate blood. Donated blood is a life-
  line for many people needing long-term treatments,
  not just in emergencies. Your blood's main compo-
  nents – red cells, plasma and platelets – are vital for
  many different uses. Go to http://www.blood.co.uk.
- Our basic compassion moves us to help needy
  people in front of us. Homeless charities such as
  Thames Reach and groups such as the Big Issue
  advise people not to give money directly to beggars, but what can you do if you see someone on the
  streets? Should you give money? Is it compassionate or callous to say hello to somebody huddled in
  a doorway, but then give them nothing? Is it patronising to offer food or coffee? Many charities suggest you offer people sleeping rough food or a drink,
  rather than money. Ask, first, what food they'd like
  to receive. But even if you don't give food or a hot or
  cold drink, do make some sort of acknowledgment.

Don't look away. That's disrespectful. Even if you're not going to give something, make eye contact and say 'No, sorry', because it's at least acknowledging that the person *is* there. In a BBC interview in 2016, a spokesman for Crisis at Christmas said: 'Whether or not people give money to beggars is a personal decision, but we know from our own clients how important a simple act of kindness can be to those in desperate circumstances.' Thames Reach says: 'By all means, engage with people on the street. Perhaps buy them food or a cup of tea. Best of all, if you are concerned for them because you think they are sleeping rough, contact the Streetlink helpline on 0300 500 0914 or go to www.streetlink.org.uk.'

In a nutshell

- Being welcoming lets people know that you're pleased they're there and that they belong. Aim to be inclusive; to enable people to feel part of something; to feel that they can be involved in what you're doing or talking about.
- In social situations, be open to small talk. It's not what you talk about – it's simply about connecting; coming across as an approachable person who is open to exchanging a few pleasantries. Imagine that the other person is already your friend. Smile, ask questions, be interested and say something about yourself.
- You have an opportunity to be generous whenever you're aware that extra effort on your part – with your time, your money, your possessions,

your energy, skills, knowledge and encouragement – could make all the difference.

- When you encourage someone, acknowledge the difficulties but point out what qualities and strengths they have that will help contribute to overcoming problems and achieving what they're aiming for.

- Get the other person to visualise what success will look and feel like. Encourage them to identify what they can do and to take it one step at a time. Don't, though, wait until they've succeeded or achieved their goal to say something positive. Acknowledge their efforts and point out what they've already achieved – that they've done so well already.

- You've got a unique set of skills, knowledge and experiences. As a mentor, you can share the knowledge, the lessons, the experiences and the skills you've accumulated.

- Use your empathy: remember what it was like when you were inexperienced in an area of your life. Be sensitive to the unique needs of others. Recognise that your circumstances and how you coped may be different for someone else.

- As an advocate, you can support someone by speaking or doing something on behalf of a person about issues that matter to them in situations where they don't feel able to say or do something for themselves.

- If something strikes you as unfair or uncalled for, have courage and speak out. A firm, polite challenge is sometimes all that is needed.

- Express appreciation to others: say thank you.
- Extend your appreciation further by acknowledging the positive difference that their actions had for you. People feel good if they know that they made a difference. So if what someone has done has had a positive effect on you, tell them; tell them how they helped or inspired you.
- Compliments and praise should also be extended to someone who has achieved or overcome something, has made a special effort or put extra time into something that's benefited someone else.
- Acknowledge personal qualities or special efforts. Compliment a person on an achievement, a job well done and on things you know they value and are proud of. Notice what someone is wearing and how they look and make a positive, appropriate comment.
- If you can't tell a person to their face, put it in writing.
- When you can, don't just express appreciation, show it. When you show appreciation for something, you demonstrate your feelings through actions. You reciprocate; you give in return.
- Make kindness a habit: do something kind every day so that after a while, kindness becomes a habit – it becomes who you are.

4
Kindness and Respect

Be non-judgmental

We're constantly judging other people's words and actions. It would be impossible not to; we're human – it's what we do – we judge, assess, form opinions and come to conclusions about others. But when we're judging – being judgmental – more often than not, rather than looking at the pros and cons, we're only looking at the negative aspects of a person or situation. We judge things that other people do that we don't approve of; the odd-looking outfit your friend is wearing, for example, or a colleague taking too long with a lunch break or the way your sister brings up her children.

Often, our judgments are about issues we find difficult to understand and sympathise with; a relative who has smoked all their life and has recently been diagnosed with lung cancer, or the friend who was sacked because he rarely showed up to work on time. (They brought it on themselves.) The unkempt and dishevelled rough sleeper (It's their choice – there are shelters for these people. Aren't there?) Your colleague who's broken her leg taking part in an extreme sport. (What can you expect if you do something so risky?) The amount your sister drinks. (She needs to get a grip.) Your teenager who got a detention for not handing his homework in on time. (He's not trying hard enough.) The tattoo your Mum regrets having done last year. (You told her it was a stupid idea – she wouldn't listen.) Your brother who is still with the partner no one in your family, including you, likes or trusts. (What *is* wrong with him?)

Too often, when we see something someone does or listen to what someone says – and we don't approve of it or agree with it – we become critical and judgmental. We have ideas of what they 'should' be doing and the way they are or are not 'supposed' to do things. We judge their choices as 'wrong'. And that's the end of it. We don't try to find out more. We don't try to understand. We don't think that they are simply managing a situation in a different way than we would.

Imagine, for example, that you bump into someone you haven't seen for a while. You're surprised to see how overweight this person has become. He tells you he hasn't been well – he has high blood pressure and has been diagnosed as borderline diabetic. He eats junk food every day and never exercises. He feels bad about himself. You make a few sympathetic noises but actually you judge this person as sad and pathetic; he's doing nothing to help himself!

The truth is, he's been depressed about his poor health. He feels fat and ugly, lonely, scared and unsupported. Because of his depression, he has no motivation to change his circumstances; he avoids thinking about his health. In fact, staying in, eating and binge-watching TV shows is the only way he knows how to cope. But you're caught up in how you think he 'should' be and what he 'should' do. You're not considering what he might be going through and why. You can't possibly help, be kind or compassionate from a place of judgment.

We all have assumptions about others that prevent us from respecting them, their situations and their choices. We assume we know the whole story. What, though, if you were able to view other people's circumstances and choices with an open mind? What if you were able to show kindness to others without thinking about whether or not they deserve some kindness? They do all deserve it.

Rather than assume and critically judge, better to be charitable; have a kindly perspective, interpretation and understanding of someone else's difficulties and challenges. But not just their difficulties; their failings and foibles, weaknesses and weirdnesses too.

Think of a time when someone did something you didn't approve of. Something that went wrong and they suffered as a result. How did you respond? What would have been a kind response from you?

Replace judgment with kindness

Be kind, for everyone you meet is fighting a harder battle.
Plato

First, you need to be aware that you're being judgmental. If someone's circumstances or actions leave you feeling irritated, impatient, disappointed or even angry with them, then you're probably being judgmental. If you think they've brought it on themselves or that they should change their ways, then you're judging them. If you're dismissive about a person's plight, then you're being judgmental. If you talk disparagingly about them and belittle them, then you're being judgmental.

Empathise

As the sun makes ice melt, kindness causes misunderstanding, mistrust, and hostility to evaporate.

Albert Schweitzer

After you catch yourself judging, ask yourself a couple of questions to see if you can understand where the person may be coming from.

- Do I really understand their situation?
- What might have caused or motivated them to do that or behave like that? What could be a reasonable explanation?
- Can I learn more about their situation?

Instead of judging someone for what they've done or failed to do, try instead to understand the person. So, your Mum regrets her tattoo. Have you asked her what appealed to her about getting a tattoo in the first place? The person sleeping rough: what do you really know about how and why a person might be a rough sleeper? There will be mitigating circumstances; circumstances which, if you knew about them, would modify your judgment. Try to imagine the circumstances that might have led to the person's situation.

Why do you think it's a problem for you? The teenager who's got a detention for not handing their homework in on time – do you feel irritated because they didn't hand the homework in on time, or because they're moaning about the detention? Be empathic. Can you empathise with the other person's feelings – the regret, for example, that someone feels for a mistake they've made – if not with their choices?

You don't have to approve of how someone is or has reacted to a situation to realise that, to a greater or lesser extent, they're having a hard time.

Remember, they are simply managing a situation in a different way than you would. You don't have to agree with how they're doing it. But show them kindness anyway; give them the benefit of the doubt. Construct the most favourable interpretation that the facts allow. Concede that a person *may* be justified in behaving the way that they do.

Challenge your assumptions and prejudices by looking for what you share with people rather than what separates you from them. Look at your own behaviour. Too often it turns out you're judging someone for something that you also do or have done. For example, the next time you're cursing someone else for their bad driving, ask yourself: 'Have I ever driven badly?' Of course you have. We all have! Have you ever not done something out of laziness, or done something because you thought it would look or feel good, but you later regretted it?

You can practise responding with kindness and empathy. Next time you read or hear – on the radio, TV or in public – someone else's opinion and it annoys you, think about giving them the benefit of the doubt. What could be a reasonable explanation for why they've done or said what they did? Believe something good about someone, rather than something bad.

Acceptance

Not only do you not need to approve, very often you don't even need to understand why someone is or isn't doing something. You just need to accept it; it is possible to accept without understanding.

Acceptance is different from tolerance. Tolerating something implies that you endure – you reluctantly put up with – something. Acceptance is a step beyond tolerance. It's kinder than tolerance. Acceptance involves recognising that something is, has been or will be. Acceptance means not trying to resist, change or control a person or a situation.

Suppose, for example, that someone told you they think that dark chocolate is better than milk chocolate. You prefer milk chocolate. Are you really going to try and persuade them that milk chocolate is better than dark chocolate? It's unlikely. What's more likely is that you'll *accept* you have different likes and dislikes.

The same accepting approach applies to other people's opinions, beliefs, feelings and responses that differ from your own. If it doesn't harm or violate you or someone else, you can choose to respect and accept their choice as valid; as having worth and value.

Being patient

Not only do people think, feel and do things differently, they may also have a different timetable than you; they may do things at a different pace. Have patience. Patience, like acceptance, is the ability and willingness to let something be; to wait calmly without having the urge to force it to be when *you* want it to be. Patience enables you to accept behaviour and situations and therefore show kindness.

Whether it's people who are physically slower than you, slower to learn or understand, or slower at expressing themselves, or describing or explaining something; too often in these situations, when we realise that something or someone is going to take longer than we'd like, we start looking for ways to hurry things up.

Having respect, patience and kindness means accepting that people and situations develop at their own speed. Maybe it's the story you've heard someone tell a hundred times already. They've told it many times before, but you don't tell them that. They enjoy reminiscing. Perhaps it's the supermarket checkout assistant chatting with a customer who has more than two or three people waiting behind them. Kindness, patience and acceptance help you to see the importance of these small exchanges between people.

Recognise when you're becoming impatient. Stop fuelling your impatience with how wrong it all is or how slow they are. If you feel yourself becoming agitated, irritated and frustrated, tell yourself 'This too will pass'. Time always passes, and how you feel during that time is of your own making. You *can* choose to be accepting, patient and kind.

Impatience rarely gets others to move faster. In fact, it can interfere with their ability to think clearly and act competently. All you're doing is creating stress for them. And that's not kind! Remind yourself that you can't help someone from a position of impatience and judgment.

Keep your mind and heart open. The world has got plenty of impatient, judgmental, unreasonable people in it, so try and be one of the kind ones.

Being tactful

Empathy, acceptance and patience all help you avoid responding unkindly to others in situations where you don't like, approve or agree with what someone is doing or how they are doing it.

What, though, if someone wants to know if you approve of something they've done or are doing? What if they actively seek your opinion? Maybe someone asked what you thought about their new hairstyle or what they were wearing. Perhaps they cooked a meal, baked a cake, gave a performance or completed a piece of work. They said they wanted your honest opinion, but you didn't know how to say it in a way that was both honest and kind.

Is it possible to turn a potentially difficult, awkward situation into an honest but kind one? Yes, by being tactful. Being tactful means having a sense of what's appropriate to say or do in any one particular situation to avoid giving offence. It's the ability to be honest in a way that considers and respects other people's abilities and feelings. It means responding with grace and consideration.

Imagine your colleague Jon has just finished giving a presentation. His presentation was badly structured and went on for too long. Jon asks for your feedback. You tell him it was OK but it was a bit confused at times and that he went on for too long. Unsurprisingly, Jon is disappointed. You feel bad; you wanted to be honest, but you didn't intend to hurt his feelings and discourage him.

In another example, your friend asks you what you think of the chocolate tart they made. You think it wasn't very good and you tell them so. Of course it's true. But is it necessary? Is it kind?

It's not just about what you say, often it's what you don't say. A helpful piece of advice here is this: before you speak, let your words pass through three gates. At the first gate, ask yourself: 'Is it true?' At the second gate ask: 'Is it necessary?' At the third gate ask: 'Is it kind?'

If it can't pass through at least two gates, it's better left unsaid.

However, while it may be kind to want to protect the feelings of someone, simply not being honest is not kind. What if you said that the presentation was good and the tart was delicious, and, later, someone else is honest and says the presentation was rubbish and the meal was tasteless? What if they then ask why you weren't honest with them when they asked you?

Giving feedback. Kindly

It's not difficult to respond with tact; with both honesty *and* kindness. You simply say what aspects were good and suggest aspects that could be improved. Tact shows respect and integrity. It helps avoid conflict and allows others to save face. Saying what aspects were good and suggesting what aspects could be improved is saying what's true, and necessary, and still being kind.

When you're giving feedback, start with the positive aspects of what they've done. For example, you could start by saying to Jon: 'You made some very good points; you obviously did a lot of research before you gave the presentation.'

Then simply say how it could be improved: 'If you were to do it again, I think your main points could be in a more logical order and you should keep the presentation to ten minutes.'

And the chocolate tart? Look at this response: 'Your tart was so chocolatey *but* it was too sweet.'

'But' is a minimising word that detracts from the positive sentence before it. Replacing the word 'but' with 'and' creates a much more positive meaning. 'And' is positive and infers there's a helpful suggestion to come. 'Your tart was so chocolatey *and* if next time you add a little less sugar, then for me it would be perfect!'

Replacing the word 'but' with 'and' is a neat little trick because the word 'and' forces you to complete the sentence in a positive way. How, for example, would you finish this feedback to someone who'd asked you what you thought of what they planned to wear to a wedding next month? You think the shoes don't match the outfit. 'I love the suit – the colour and fit are great *and* if ... then the whole look will be perfect!'

For any one issue, though, do limit your suggestions; limit them to two aspects that could be improved. Any more than two and you risk discouraging and demoralising the other person.

What, though, if it's too late for changes or improvements? Supposing a friend asks you what you think of what they're wearing and it's too late to change anything about it now. Or they ask you what you think of their new haircut. In that case, find something positive about it – the colour, the fit, the length, the fabric – that you honestly like and just leave it at that. That's saying only what's necessary, it's true *and* it's kind.

Giving criticism. Kindly

If, however, you *have* to tell someone they've done something wrong – that they've failed to do something or have done it wrong or incorrectly – how do you say so without hurting their feelings, or making them defensive or angry? Nobody likes being told that they're behaving, acting, looking or saying things the wrong way, but just because people don't like being criticised doesn't mean you shouldn't.

Often, if you don't speak up, if you suppress your irritation and frustration and if you hold back the criticism, your resentment can build up and can leak out in other ways. And it probably won't come out kindly! It's not easy but it is possible to give criticism with kindness; with tact and good intentions. Just like kind, honest feedback, kind, honest criticism is constructive. It involves giving a specific, positive suggestion.

Before you say anything, decide what, exactly, it is that the other person has done that's 'wrong'. Then think about what change or improvement you want to see.

Consider, for example, this criticism: 'You've loaded the dishwasher all wrong! I've just had to reload it. Why can't you do it like I asked?' That might be honest and true, but it's not kind. It's not constructive. Constructive criticism describes what can be changed or improved. A better approach would be: 'Thanks for loading the dishwasher. I rearranged the plates and bowls so that the dirty sides face the water spray. Could you do it like that next time so that they get completely clean?'

In another example, to a friend who rarely turns up on time: 'I get wound up every time you turn up late.' (Saying what the problem is.) 'Can you just text me when you're leaving home, then I'll know when to expect you?' (Saying what changes you want.)

And to a colleague who constantly interrupts others at a meeting, instead of saying 'Shut up! Stop interrupting people!', you simply say what you want to happen: 'Please let the other person finish what they're saying.'

Letting someone down/disappointing them

Your manager asks you to take on some extra work; you don't want to. Your brother asks you to have his children for a long weekend; you dread the thought but you don't want to let him down. Another parent asks you to help raise money for the school; you don't have the time. A neighbour wants to come round in the evening for a chat and a bottle of wine; you're too tired. Someone at a party asks you for your professional advice; you don't want to think about work at a party. A family member really wants you to spend Christmas with them; you've already decided to go away for Christmas.

Have there been similar situations and times when you've wanted to say no, to refuse to do something, but you've struggled to know how to let them down without hurting their feelings? To say no without feeling guilty?

You do have a right to say no! You can empathise – understand that they're disappointed – but remember, you can't be totally responsible for other people's situations and feelings. Saying yes to anything and everything others ask you to do is people pleasing: doing things just to avoid upsetting them and hurting their feelings, rather than because you genuinely want to make things easier or help out.

However, although you can't avoid their disappointment, you can say no and let other people down gently and kindly. You can offer a compromise: something in between or a variation of what they want that you can't or don't want to do.

First, though, you'll need to say no. Don't waffle or give lots of excuses. You don't need to explain why you won't do something, you only need one valid reason. Make your explanation honest and short.

'Thanks for thinking of me and asking me to help out with the fundraising for the children's school, Natalie. I've got too many other commitments this year.' Then offer an alternative. 'How about asking Sean? He's a new parent to the school and he might be pleased to be asked and included.'

Is the request something you would consider at another time? If so, tell them. 'I've got too many commitments this year but do please ask me again next year; I should be more free to get involved with fundraising then.' Or offer a compromise, saying what you can do instead. 'I'd be happy to donate something to the raffle.'

And with the other examples? When someone wants to chat or come over and you're busy, or you're tired and don't want to be sociable: 'Hello Amir! I'm sorry I can't invite you in now. How about we text each other tomorrow and arrange to get together next week?'

When someone wants your professional advice: 'In brief, my advice is … But if you'd like to talk more about this, you could text or email me for an appointment sometime soon.'

To your brother: 'I'm not able to babysit. But I'd like to see the kids. Can you join us for lunch next Sunday?'

To your manager: 'I can't/don't want to do that. I can find someone else who will – would that help?'

And finally, to the relative: 'We're going away for Christmas. How about we get together on New Year's Day?'

If the other person persists and isn't taking no for an answer, calmly acknowledge what they've said but stand your ground. 'I know you're disappointed. Sorry. But as I said, instead I can …'

Giving bad news

Although giving feedback and criticism and letting someone down kindly relies on you saying something positive
and constructive, giving someone bad news rarely has
positive aspects to it.

Whether it's telling a colleague that their project isn't
going ahead, having to fire someone, telling someone
that you've lost or broken something that belongs to
them – often, it can be just as hard for you, the person
giving the bad news, as it is for the person receiving it.
How and when to tell them? What if they get upset and
start crying? How will you manage that? What if they're
annoyed and start sulking or getting angry? What if they
blame you; hold you completely responsible for what's
happened?

Sometimes, in some situations, it's tempting to put off
telling the bad news in the hope that things will change
or improve or they'll find out some other way. That
way you can put it off altogether. But holding back
because you can't handle the other person's reaction or
your embarrassment could just serve to compound the
problem.

Be honest, don't withhold information out of fear, or to
save face. Withholding information can lead someone to
misunderstand or underestimate the problem/bad news.

Imagine a situation where, thinking you were being kind,
you withheld some information from a friend, family

member or colleague – a difficult truth, something that might upset, frighten or worry them. If and when you think that withholding some information from another person is being kind, ask yourself whether it also shows respect to the other person, as an equal – with a right to know anything that would affect them, capable of managing their emotions and reactions and capable of making decisions with regards to the truth of the situation.

Have courage! You *can* give bad news with honesty and kindness.

First, when you have bad news to deliver, know that you must lay it out plainly; the other person needs to be clear about the situation. If you can, prepare what you're going to say. It's also helpful to anticipate the reaction and questions the other person might have.

Consider the setting. There's never a great moment to pass on bad news, but you may be able to find the least terrible time. The place, too, can make a difference: it should offer some privacy, allow the other person to react without feeling embarrassed about being upset.

If you need to give the news right away, you can say 'I need to talk with you about … '. This at least gives them some warning instead of you just blurting out the news.

Briefly explain what's led to the situation. Setting the context – the circumstances relevant to the issue – can make a difference to how the bad news is grasped and understood. For example: 'I was in all day but in the evening I realised I hadn't seen Mitzi, your cat. (Setting the context.) I don't know how, but somehow she's got out and I can't find her.' Here's another example, to a young person working for a few hours on a Saturday in a local corner shop. First, the context: 'Since the new year, we haven't been so busy.' Then, the bad news, simply and honestly: 'I'm sorry, I'm not going to be able to keep you on. Next Saturday will have to be your last.'

Be prepared with concise and credible answers to the other person's questions: 'Wasn't I working hard enough?' Or 'What do you mean, you don't know how the cat got out? Have you looked all over the house?'

Once it seems like the bad news has sunk in and you've answered their questions, there may still be something positive you can say. Think about this before you tell them the bad news. However, that hope must be grounded in reality.

For example, to the young person who is no longer going to be working at the shop: 'If things pick up, I'll give you a call and see if you're free to work for me again. If you find something else in the meantime, I'd be happy to give you a very good reference. You're hard working and friendly to the customers. Thank you, I've really appreciated it.'

And in the case of the lost cat, state what more you can do to help; what possible steps to take next. Focus on what can be done rather than what can't be done. 'I want to do whatever I can to help find her – do you want to check the house and I'll go and ask the neighbours if they've seen her?'

Bad news without ideas for solutions is truly bad news!

Be empathic: listen to the other person; let them talk. Listen and acknowledge what they say and how they feel. Acknowledge their distress: 'I know you're worried we won't find Mitzi. I'm sorry you're so upset.' An empathic response acknowledges not only someone's feelings but also the reasons for those feelings.

Don't say 'I know just how you feel', or 'Try not to worry about it'. Although you might mean well, the other person might feel that you don't understand or you're attempting to minimise the situation.

In a nutshell

- We often struggle to respect and accept other people's choices, beliefs and abilities as valid and worthy. We judge and make assumptions about things that other people do that we don't approve of, that we don't understand or sympathise with.
- Replace your assumptions and judgments with kindness. Aim to be charitable; have a kindly perspective, interpretation and understanding of someone else's difficulties and challenges, their failings and foibles, weaknesses and weirdnesses.
- Other people are simply managing a situation in a different way than you would. Empathise. You

don't have to agree with how they're doing it, but show them kindness anyway; give them the benefit of the doubt. Construct the most favourable interpretation that the facts allow. Concede that a person *may* be justified in behaving the way that they do.

- Challenge your assumptions and prejudices by looking for what you share with people rather than what separates you from them.
- Not only do you not need to approve, very often you don't even need to understand why someone is or isn't doing something. You just need to accept; it is possible to accept without understanding.
- If it doesn't harm or violate you or someone else, you can choose to respect and accept their choice as valid; as having worth and value.
- Have patience. Patience can help you accept that people and situations develop at their own speed.
- Remind yourself that you can't help someone from a position of impatience and judgment.
- Being tactful is being honest in a way that considers and respects other people's abilities and feelings. Tact shows respect and integrity. It helps avoid conflict and allows others to save face.
- It's not difficult to respond with tact; with both honesty *and* kindness. You simply say what aspects were good and suggest aspects that could be improved.
- Although you can't avoid other people's disappointment, you can say no and let them down gently and kindly. You can offer a compromise, an alternative: something in between or a variation of what they want that you can't or don't want to do.

- Have courage! You *can* give bad news with honesty and kindness. Lay it out plainly; if you can, prepare what you're going to say. Set the context: briefly explain what's led to the situation. Anticipate the reaction and questions the other person might have.
- Say what, if anything, you can do to help. Focus on what can be done rather than what can't be done.
- Be empathic: listen to the other person; let them talk. Don't say 'I know just how you feel', or 'Try not to worry about it'. Listen and acknowledge what they say and how they feel.

5

Be Kind When Others are Rude and Inconsiderate

Treat everyone with kindness and respect. Not because they are nice, but because you are.

Author unknown

A few years ago, writer and teacher Arthur Rosenfeld was in a 'drive-thru' queue at a Starbucks in Florida. The man in the car behind him was getting impatient and angry, leaning on his horn and shouting insults at both Arthur and the Starbucks workers.

Arthur looked in the rearview mirror. The face of the impatient driver behind him was twisted with anger. 'I'll show you what happens to rude and impatient people,' thought Arthur. But then he caught himself; he refocused his eyes and noticed that his own face didn't look much different.

In one moment Arthur had what he calls a 'change of consciousness'; he chose to keep calm and change the negativity into something positive. Arthur paid for both his own coffee and the other man's order and then he went on his way. When he got home at the end of the day, Arthur discovered that his actions had featured on the national news. Within twenty-four hours, through social media, it had spread around the world.

No doubt you too have met mean, rude people. It could be that they were simply inconsiderate: they weren't thinking about the effect of their words or actions on you; using the last of anything and not replacing it – the paper in the copier at work, petrol in a shared car or the loo paper at home. Maybe, though, it was someone speaking over you or interrupting before you'd finished speaking. Perhaps they casually dismissed your opinion on a matter. It could've been someone blocking the aisle in the supermarket or reaching past you for something on a shelf. Perhaps they jumped the queue at the checkout.

Why are people rude?

Mostly, when someone is rude – thoughtless and inconsiderate – it probably just happened in the moment. They didn't make a conscious decision to be rude and mean; they didn't wake up in the morning and think, 'Today, I am going to be rude and horrible'. They didn't know they were being rude; they weren't thinking – they were just being thoughtless and inconsiderate. Maybe they were stressed, they were in a hurry, or feeling left out or ignored. Perhaps, though, they *were* being deliberately mean – impatient with you or deliberately dismissing, ignoring or excluding you – or their rudeness is a habit: it's the way they usually interact with the world.

Whatever the reason for their behaviour, it's not easy to respond kindly. Often, when others are inconsiderate, rude or even hostile, we assume the worst and either defend or attack. But often that just sets up a new cycle of rudeness and resentment. What to do? How can you – like Arthur Rosenfeld – have a 'change of consciousness'? How do you avoid being rude and unkind back? By forgiving.

The problem with forgiveness, though, is that so often it feels like you're giving in and letting the other person off; letting them get away with their rudeness.

Forgiving

Even if it's a relatively small thing – a friend or colleague not calling to say they'll be late, or someone texting or checking social media during a meeting or a meal, or the cashier at the petrol station who not only didn't acknowledge you but continued to talk on their phone as you paid – it's not always easy to think kindly and forgive the other person.

There's much sentimentalising of forgiveness. The idea that forgiveness involves letting the other person off and having kindly feelings towards someone who has annoyed or upset you in some way is idealistic; it gets in the way of understanding the real thing.

Forgiveness is first and foremost for your benefit, not the person who hurt or offended you. Forgiveness means recognising that you've already been annoyed, irritated or embarrassed once, you don't need to let the offence and the hurt burden you by holding onto it.

Forgiving someone isn't letting them off, it's simply letting go; letting go of the resentment, frustration or anger that you feel, putting someone else's actions behind you and moving on. Whether or not the other person has apologised, there's no point in tormenting yourself any further.

Forgiveness doesn't mean you'll respond kindly, but it does prevent you from responding unkindly. Forgiveness means you avoid being as rude or as inconsiderate as the other person has been.

Suspend judgment

Try to keep an overall positive impression of others and keep their negative behaviour in the larger context of their good nature. With this perspective you will be in a much better position to respond with forgiveness and positivity.

Don't let rudeness make you respond with more of the same. The best way to defuse rude, obviously bad behaviour – a sudden loss of temper, a wild accusation, a very mean remark – is to stay open, giving the other person a chance to calm down and adjust their behaviour to match yours. Give them the benefit of the doubt. Look for reasonable explanations. Assume that if they're deliberately being rude they're just having a bad day and taking it out on the world.

Empathise

Empathise – look for the feelings behind the rudeness. The other person may be stressed, worried or upset – conditions that usually invite sympathy rather than offence. You can make a difference by recognising their rudeness as a sign that, one way or another, they may be having a difficult day and being kind.

Remember that sometimes the rude person is you! Maybe not today, but there will have been times when you were rude and inconsiderate. And you're not a bad person. So next time somebody's rude to you, remember that one incident of rudeness doesn't mean they're a bad person either.

Like Arthur Rosenfeld, you can often disarm difficult people by responding in unexpected ways. In the face of a tirade, instead of attacking or getting defensive, make a kind gesture. Imagine, for example, someone snaps at you because, whether it's your fault or not, they're disappointed they haven't got what they want or they're annoyed that a problem hasn't been resolved in the way they expected it to be. Consider offering help. Often, a person who's rude and horrible is so because they feel frustrated, thwarted or disappointed about something. If there's something you can do to resolve their frustration, you may see them switch from rudeness to gratitude and appreciation.

However, do know when to let it go. If you can make an appropriate, kind gesture to the other person, go ahead. But if they reject it or if the person is getting het up – more rude and aggressive – walk away.

Consider who you're dealing with. You may not be dealing with a stable person; they may be so stressed out they could flip at any time. Do or say one wrong thing and things could get worse. So, it may be better to say nothing, excuse yourself and move away. Maya Angelou once said: 'When someone shows you who they are, believe them the first time.' She's right; the last thing you want is to get yourself into trouble.

Don't sweat the small stuff!

In fact, often, doing nothing is not just the safest thing, it's also the kindest thing you can do. The cashier at the petrol station who not only didn't acknowledge you but continued to talk on their phone as you paid? Accept it. Then let it go!

Accept what has happened – you can't change it. It is what it is.

Get things into perspective; does it really matter that your partner snaps at you for not putting the lid back on a jar of jam properly? Or that you forgot to put the papers in the recycling. Do you need to retaliate when a colleague corrects you if you commit a word crime – if you use words like 'defo' and 'obvs'? Or say 'basically' or 'actually' a lot?

Do nothing. Say nothing. Kindness and respect are not just about what you do – they're also about what you don't do, what you hold back from doing.

Sometimes it's better to hold back on your opinions and avoid arguments than provoke a row amongst good friends or at a family event, for example. Perhaps there's nothing to be gained from arguing with your uncle about gay marriage. Ask yourself: 'Is it really worth losing my cool over this? Is it worth even engaging with this person? Will it be worth spoiling a family occasion?' Be kind and considerate to everyone else; avoid a row.

Maybe their values oppose yours; yes, it's hard to respect people who are rude or insulting. Aim, though, to avoid being unkind even if they won't do the same. Remember, before you speak, ask yourself: is it kind, is it necessary, is it true? Does it improve on the silence?

When someone's rudeness upsets you, take a moment to breathe. Count to three. Literally. You should do this. If you don't react immediately to what they have said or done, you will give yourself a better chance of choosing your response. And your response can be to do nothing.

People do often realise when their comment has been stonewalled. When you don't react – don't agree or disagree, don't nod, shake your head, don't even say 'mmm' – people know. Their rudeness is not your fault. Let them find their own solutions.

Then, removing yourself from the situation is the surest way to avoid more rude behaviour from the same person.

Be assertive, not unkind

This doesn't mean to say that you should be a pushover; it doesn't mean you have to put up with inconsiderate behaviour. You can still assert your position and stand up for yourself. You do have a choice.

What if, for example, you want to say something to the friend or colleague texting or checking social media during a meeting or meal? Or you want to respond to your partner or teenager who snaps at you about something while you're both out shopping?

If someone else's rudeness or lack of consideration crosses the line and needs to be addressed, how do you say something firmly without being unkind? As witty and clever as responses such as 'I don't know what your problem is, but I'll bet it's hard to pronounce' or 'I see you've set aside this special time to humiliate yourself in public' are, the aim is not to handle rudeness with rudeness!

Simply respond firmly and concisely. Use short, truthful statements: 'That wasn't nice' or 'I don't like that'. Or 'I don't think that's appropriate'. Or 'I feel hurt/upset by what you did/said. Please don't do that again.'

You don't need to elaborate. You don't need to explain. You just need to say you don't like it, it's not true, it's inappropriate, and so on.

To a rude comment about your ability or appearance, you can simply reply, 'Right. Okay.' To a rude or intrusive question, you could say: 'I don't want to answer that, so let's talk about something else.' And change the subject.

If they make another comment, you can say nothing or you can respond in a way that will both acknowledge what they've said but also confirm you're standing strong. Say, for example, they retaliate with 'You're being ridiculous'. You would respond with: 'You might think I'm being ridiculous (acknowledging) but I don't like that/think it's appropriate' (standing firm). Then change the subject or excuse yourself and walk away.

You'll need courage and kindness in the face of rudeness and humiliation. In Disney's 2015 remake of *Cinderella*, Cinderella's mother, before she died, told Cinderella that she wanted to share with her 'a great secret that will see you through all the trials life has to offer'. The secret? 'Have courage and be kind.' Courage enables you to face difficulty *despite* your fear and concerns. Courage is strength in the face of hostility.

Kindness in the face of criticism

What, though, if someone says something that's not just inconsiderate or rude, but highly critical?

Direct criticisms can come from anyone: a family member, friend, colleague or a complete stranger. Maybe it's someone who is always firing off and always finds something wrong. Perhaps, though, it comes from nowhere and catches you by surprise.

For many of us, when we're criticised, it's hard not to react instantly. To shut down; sulk, feel guilty or embarrassed; or to attack – snap back or vehemently defend yourself. Of course, your response is dependent on who it is, why, where and when they're criticising you. But whatever and whoever, there is a way to handle criticism without being rude and unkind. You *can* be the better person; the kinder person.

Count to three and then ask yourself: is it true? Sure, it may be rude and mean, but in most criticisms you can find a few grains of truth. Here's an example of a time I managed to respond positively to a criticism: someone wrote a review of my book *How to Deal with Difficult People* which ended by saying 'In truth I doubt the author has ever dealt with a snarling customer'. My response?

Thanks for giving me an opportunity to clarify your comment that it's unlikely I've ever dealt with a snarling customer. I now realise I should've said something about my experiences with difficult people in the introduction to the book.

In my working life – from waiting tables as a teenager, to all the years of experience teaching, tutoring and coaching, plus my more recent experiences of leading walking holidays – I've dealt with 'difficult people'. Whether it was a customer complaining about their coffee not being hot enough, a student unhappy with their grade, or a bird hunter with a gun threatening me and others if we insisted on our right to continue on the path we were walking, I've certainly had my fair share of snarling customers!

By thanking the critic, taking it as an opportunity to clarify, and being positive, I have, I think, accepted the criticism and shown goodwill. (Even though my first reaction was to reply with rudeness and an insult!)

As Michelle Obama said during the 2016 presidential elections which Donald Trump won: 'When they go low, you go high.'

If you choose to respond to a criticism, do the same; surprise them with kindness. Imagine, for example, someone said to you: 'Your haircut looks ridiculous – why don't you just go to a proper barbers?' Does it? Is it possible that getting your partner to cut your hair means it looks … well, if not ridiculous, then certainly not its best?

Instead of reacting immediately by defending yourself or going on the attack, stop. Stop and ask yourself: could there be any truth in the criticism? Maybe there is some truth, but let's suppose you can't afford to get your hair cut professionally. You might want to tell them that. You might respond by saying 'You're right, it probably would look better if I had it cut at a barbers. I can't afford to go regularly though.'

If they haven't said so already, ask the other person what they suggest you do. You might agree with their solution or you might not.

If you honestly feel that their criticism is unfair and invalid, say so. Calmly acknowledge what they think – 'I know you think my haircut looks ridiculous, but … '. Or say nothing and let it go. Most likely their mind is already made up and nothing you say will change it.

Shutting someone up. Kindly

We've all come across people who, even if they're not being rude or critical, repeat the same stories and anecdotes or talk about topics in needless detail. Maybe you know someone who always manages to bring the conversation back to themselves? Or you know someone who complains and moans or brags and boasts.

People who talk too much or are negative, dull and boring usually fail to recognise the frustrated, resentful feelings of their listeners. Typically, you, the listener, get so bored or wound up you either stop listening altogether or you get so irritated and frustrated that your resentment builds and you react harshly and rudely.

Can you get someone to stop talking without feeling and appearing rude? Yes. There *are* ways to do it kindly.

If you know someone is a talker, and you'll have a hard time getting away, state early on that you can't stop for long. You could say 'Great to see you, but I only have a few minutes to talk'. 'Right now is not a great time to talk, let's catch up another time. Maybe you could text me a date/time that you're free.'

But if you do have to stay put, rather than switch off, listen. Listening for a reasonable amount of time might tell you why they are talking so much. While some people talk a lot because they're self-centred, some people talk because they are nervous or have something bothering or upsetting them. It's not always obvious, but if that is the case – if they're bothered about something – you can decide whether to drop everything and listen or suggest a more convenient time to listen and talk with them.

If, though, the other person just seems to like the sound of their own voice, by listening and closely following what they've said, you can pick up on it and then take the subject in a different direction or bring the 'conversation' to a close.

Be ready to jump in. Make eye contact and say their name. Stand up if you were sitting down. When the other person takes a breath or in the brief moment when they finish a sentence, interrupt by saying their name and in a firm but calm tone say: 'I'd like to say something … ', or 'I'm just going to interrupt … ', or 'I'm going to stop you there … '.

Add some experience of your own that will confirm that you've listened to what they've told you and, at the same time, allow you to take control of the conversation.

For example: 'Well Lewis, it sounds like you made the right decision to leave your job and work freelance ... ' and before he can say anything else, change the subject. Just go straight into it without drawing breath: ' ... I've sometimes thought of doing the same but I do enjoy my job at Smith and Jones, although I've often wanted to ... ' and take the conversation where you want it to go. If you then want to get away, just continue by saying 'Well I've got to get on now ... '.

Widen the circle. If you're in a group, try directing questions to someone else. Say, for example: 'Amy, Lewis has been telling me that going freelance was the best thing he ever did. What do you think; have you ever thought of going freelance?' Or you might say: 'Lewis, do come with me, I want to introduce you to Josh/go to the bar/get some food.' This tactic makes them feel included and gives you the chance to take your leave.

Be nice. You'll feel OK about ending the conversation and the other person will be happier to let you go if you say something kind and positive. 'Thanks, you've given me some useful tips. I'll certainly remember them if I do ever decide to go freelance!' Or simply say 'It's been great talking to you, but I am going to go now'.

Have limits. Telling someone to 'shut up', even politely, is not easy. But if someone is being offensive, aggressive, or even taking too much of your time, you need to take a stand for yourself. If you are constantly being talked over, recognise that you must be more direct. Have courage! Make eye contact and speak clearly. Raise your voice if you need to be heard, but try to keep your tone level and steady. Or excuse yourself and walk away.

How to end a friendship. Kindly

What, though, if it's not a conversation you want to get out of? What if it's actually a friendship? Maybe you have a friendship that's wearing you down or you feel your relationship is entirely one-sided. If you want to cut the cord, you *can* do it with grace and kindness.

Liv and Maria, for example, first became friends when they joined the same choir ten years ago. In the last couple of years, it seems to Liv that Maria talks mostly about her own life – she rarely asks Liv about hers. When they last met with their mutual friends, Maria told them that her daughter Ellie had just come out as gay and introduced her new, much older girlfriend to Maria. Liv exclaimed 'Gosh, I bet you didn't expect that! How do you feel about your daughter being with a woman?' It probably wasn't the most sensitive thing to say. Maria later emailed Liv: 'It was unnecessary for you to say that; you're insensitive. I'm very worried about Ellie and I don't need your stupid, crass comments.'

Liv was taken aback. She thought it through and realised that yes, she had not said the right thing exactly. But Liv also realised that, unlike meeting up with other friends who she looked forward to seeing, she actually felt a real reluctance each time she was due to meet with Maria.

She felt sad about it, but Liv knew it was time to stop trying to make it work and to let go of their friendship. But how to do it kindly?

Liv decided to stop calling and let things drift. She wouldn't confront Maria and tell her that she no longer wanted to be friends. It might be true, but she felt it wasn't necessary or kind. Instead, she quietly withdrew. She started by making excuses for not meeting up, then, as the months went by, she told Maria that she had a lot on and would contact Maria when she was freer. But Liv never did call Maria.

Whether it's because you realise you can't stand to see someone ever again, the friendship has run its course – you no longer have anything in common – or you simply don't have the time for that friendship, unless you want a full-on confrontation, aim to withdraw kindly and gracefully with as little distress and as few hurt feelings as possible. Let it fade. Rather than abruptly stop calling, texting or emailing, slowly let contact diminish.

Try not returning every phone call and don't initiate plans to meet up. Take your time to return texts and emails or don't reply at all. Say you're busy or have other reasons not to accept invitations to get together.

Do try and keep your excuses as honest as possible – don't say you've got to spend a lot of time with your mother who is unwell if that's not true. But if you do have a lot going on with family members, your children, work or travel and holidays and so on, then use that as a more general but honest reason.

Although fading out a friendship in this way avoids direct confrontation and minimises hurt feelings, it can take a while and requires an element of dishonesty, which can feel uncomfortable. The alternative, however, is harder and harsher. For example: 'Look Donald, I just don't want to be your friend. I don't agree with your values and your politics. I have neither the time or the energy for you, so I'm letting you go.'

You don't have to be unkind about it though. Don't dump three years' worth of resentment on their lap. Just explain that you've been hurt, disappointed, let down by your friendship and you're calling it a day. Sure, they might react harshly, but simply acknowledge what they've said, then repeat what you've said and move on. If, for example, Maria had told Liv she no longer wanted to be friends with her, Liv, in response, could say: 'Okay, I understand that you think I'm insensitive and I often say the wrong thing. But I feel like I can't be myself when I'm with you and that you hardly ever seem to be interested in what's going on in my life. I'm sad about it but I'd rather we don't see each other anymore.'

In a nutshell

- When others are inconsiderate, rude or even hostile, it's not easy to respond kindly. We assume the worst and typically either defend ourselves or attack. But often that just sets up a new cycle of rudeness and resentment.

- Forgiving someone isn't letting them off, it's simply letting go; letting go of the resentment, frustration or anger that you feel.
- Try to keep an overall positive impression of others and keep their negative behaviour in the larger context of their good nature. Give them the benefit of the doubt. Look for reasonable explanations. Assume that if they're deliberately being rude they're just having a bad day and taking it out on the world.
- There will have been times when you were rude and inconsiderate. And you're not a bad person. Next time somebody's rude to you, remember that one incident of rudeness doesn't mean they're a bad person either.
- Empathise; look for the feelings behind someone's rudeness. They may be stressed, worried or upset, feel thwarted or disappointed; conditions that usually invite sympathy rather than offence. If you can respond with kindness, you may see them switch from rudeness to gratitude and appreciation.
- Know when to let it go. If you can make an appropriate, kind gesture to the other person, go ahead. But if they reject it or if the person is getting het up – more rude and aggressive – walk away.
- Sometimes it's better to hold back and avoid arguments. Do nothing. Say nothing. Kindness and respect are not just about what you do, they're also about what you don't do – what you hold back from doing.

- If you do choose to respond, be assertive, not unkind. You just need to say you don't like what someone did or said; that it's not true, it's inappropriate and so on.
- If they make another comment, you can say nothing, or acknowledge what they've said but repeat that you don't like it. Then change the subject or excuse yourself and walk away.
- Instead of reacting immediately to a criticism, ask yourself if there could be any truth in it. If the criticism is unfair and invalid, say so. Or say nothing and let it go. Most likely their mind is already made up and nothing you say will change it.
- There *are* ways get someone to stop talking without being rude; to close a conversation kindly. Listen closely so that you can be ready to jump in and take the subject in a different direction.
- If you want to end a friendship, aim to do it kindly and gracefully with as little distress and as few hurt feelings as possible. Let it fade. Rather than abruptly stop calling, texting or emailing, slowly let contact diminish.
- If you do tell them why you are ending the friendship, don't be unkind about it. Just explain that you've been hurt, disappointed, let down or whatever by your friendship and you're calling it a day.

PART 2

Being Kind to Yourself

6
Don't Be So Hard on Yourself; Be Kind

How often do you give yourself a hard time when you make a mistake or you screw up? Do you feel really bad if you think you've upset someone else or let someone down? Perhaps you still feel guilty for something you said or did to someone else. Do you blame yourself if things don't turn out the way you hoped? Or maybe you take on too much – you're stressed and exhausted – but feel you should be able to cope. Does the disapproving voice inside your head leave you feeling inadequate and hopeless? When you look at social media – Twitter, Instagram and Facebook – do you ever think that everyone else is living a lovely life, compare your situation with theirs and find yours wanting? Do you doubt yourself, your abilities and your achievements?

As my American friend says, 'How's *that* been workin' for ya?'

Berating and blaming yourself when things aren't going well isn't exactly uplifting; it doesn't provide you with what you need most: kindness, hope and encouragement.

Things change, but throughout your life *you* are the one constant. You're the only one person in the world that you'll always have a relationship with. That's why it is important that you treat yourself kindly through all the ups and downs that happen; treat yourself like a life-long friend, with the same kindness and care, respect and support you would give a good friend that you care about.

Being kind – taking care of yourself – isn't about being selfish and self-centred; it isn't about letting yourself off the hook whenever you screw up. Self-kindness isn't self-pity either. Self-pity is being stuck in a state of 'poor me'. Self-kindness and compassion are more empowering. Yes, self-kindness and compassion allow you to feel sad for yourself, to feel bad because of tough times, mistakes and struggles. But self-kindness and compassion encourage you to do something constructive to make things better; to improve your situation.

Continually berating yourself with 'I'm so bad', 'I'm terrible', 'I'm worthless', being stuck in guilt, shame or regret; *that* is self-pity – it can tip over into being self-absorbed and self-centred. Just as you can't help others from a position of judgment, you can't help yourself – or anyone else – when you're stuck in self-judgment.

On the other hand, when you're kind and understanding to yourself, you recognise that it's human to fail, to make mistakes and to struggle at times. Yes, you can regret your mistakes and failures, but you're not totally consumed by them, because you're doing what you can to make things easier for yourself and that allows you to have room for others.

So how can you be kind to yourself when you've made a mistake, done something wrong, maybe done something that's offended someone else? How do you find the right balance between taking responsibility for your wrongdoing and self-compassion? Just like kindness and compassion to others, there's a number of aspects to self-kindness; aspects such as self-respect, empathy and perspective, courage, acceptance and patience, forgiveness, gratitude and appreciation.

Respect yourself

Just as kindness to others involves showing respect, kindness to yourself involves *self*-respect. Self-respect allows you to feel equal, it means knowing that, like everyone else, your needs and wishes, beliefs and opinions, efforts, abilities and contributions have worth and value. So do your rights, differences and limits have worth and value – they are as legitimate as anyone else's.

Self-respect is believing that you are good and worthy of being treated well – not just by other people, but by yourself too – even when you screw up, make mistakes, don't achieve or do well in some areas of your life.

Self-respect doesn't depend on being perfect; on never doing anything wrong. Self-respect means understanding that you're human, that it's human to have flaws and failings, but that they don't completely define you. Self-respect requires a sense of perspective.

Self-empathy and perspective

Whether you snap at your colleague or partner, yell at the kids, you fail an exam, get drunk and trip over and break your leg, or you made a pig's ear of your presentation at work today, it helps if you can gain a bit of perspective. Gaining perspective means getting a sense of where what you did or didn't do fits into the greater scheme of things. It's empathising with yourself – it's taking a step back from yourself and seeing yourself through different eyes; from someone else's kindly perspective – responding to yourself with the same understanding as a good friend would give you for what you did or didn't do.

Perspective helps you to understand that as bad as you feel about what you did or didn't or can't do, you need to put it in context; take into account all the circumstances or facts that surround a particular situation that you're giving yourself a hard time about.

Supposing, for example, you regret something you did or said. Perhaps you regret telling someone what you really thought of them; maybe you regret that you took a job, had another drink or piece of cake. Conversely, you might regret something you *didn't* do or say; you didn't say sorry, you didn't sign up for the charity run, you failed to stand up for yourself or support someone else, you didn't take that job or you regret not finishing a relationship sooner.

Consider the circumstances at the time you did or didn't do something. Maybe you had no way of knowing what the consequences would be; perhaps you were under pressure and stressed or had other commitments or limited support when you did or didn't do or say something. Maybe you misunderstood or didn't know all the facts about a situation. Be kind to yourself; know that whatever it was, you did it based on what you knew or were able to do at the time.

And if it was something you didn't do, know now that not doing something was also based on the circumstances and conditions at the time. Perhaps, for example, you failed to speak up for or support someone else. Maybe, at the time, you were too involved with your own concerns, or you didn't realise they needed your support or you didn't want to get too involved.

That doesn't make your action or inaction right or wrong. It doesn't excuse what you did. It just explains why you did or didn't do something. You had good reasons at the time. Now you know or feel differently. What we can handle varies from day to day. It's easy in hindsight to see the realities, possibilities or requirements of a situation, or decision, after it happened.

Take responsibility and learn from it

That's not to say that you don't take responsibility for whatever it is. Taking responsibility means you accept what you did or didn't do. Nothing can change that. But what *can* change is what happens next. Learn from it, act differently next time. And if you've hurt or offended someone else, you do what you can to make amends.

Of course, 'negative' emotions such as regret and remorse, guilt and shame don't feel nice. They're not meant to feel nice! They're there for a good reason though; to prompt you to do something – something positive. 'Negative' emotions are only negative if you become stuck in berating yourself for your wrongdoing.

The kindest thing to do for yourself – and for someone else if your wrongdoing affected them – is to put it right or make up for it. Then move on. The unkindest thing you can do is to continue to berate or punish yourself in some way. That's not helping you or anyone else. It's tiresome and annoying. Get over yourself! Stop wallowing in self-blame and recrimination. Allow yourself some kindness; some empathy and understanding.

Self-acceptance

Kindness and compassion for yourself and for others both stem from the same thing: understanding the human condition. As human beings, we have all got weaknesses; we all have imperfections. Ignoring or denying that you have flaws and faults would be deluded and conceited. But dwelling on your failings and foibles isn't kind and doesn't help build self-respect. Quite the opposite! Berating yourself for your shortcomings is a surefire way to make you feel bad about yourself.

You know that telling a friend that they don't compare well with someone else or berating them for their short-comings would be unkind. So why do that to yourself? Be a kind and supportive friend to yourself instead. Give yourself a break where you fall short and accept that in some things you're a bit crap. Recognise that, more often than not, good enough is good enough. Even no good at all – because we're all no good at all at many things – can be OK. Really.

Take a reality check; knowing you simply can't do and be anything and everything is the only realistic response to the things you can't change, the talents and looks you weren't born with, the skills you're unlikely to acquire.

Accept yourself. Think of things you don't like. I don't like sushi. I can accept that. If you don't like sushi and can accept it, then you can accept that, like me, you're not very tidy, for example, or any good at concentrating on any one thing for long periods of time.

I accept that I'm never going to visit Thailand or Vietnam. I'm just not that interested. I like reality TV shows: 'I'm a Celebrity' and 'First Dates', but I've never watched 'Game of Thrones' even though everyone told me I should. I think some chat shows are overrated; I'm not that bothered about going to watch the team my husband supports: Brighton and Hove Albion. I'm hopeless at playing any sport. I'm impatient. I'm not that tidy (have I mentioned that?). I can accept all of that.

Just like me, your likes and dislikes, failings and foibles are all just part of who you are. Stop trying to be perfect. Stop with the 'I'm not enough; I'm not good enough/clever enough/strong enough/attractive enough' type of self-talk and replace it with 'I am enough. Tomorrow I can strive to be more, but right now, I'm enough.'

Rather than berate yourself, accept yourself. Of course, if you want to, you can still do better. Acknowledge your potential and aim to improve, just one step at a time.

Avoid the comparison trap

Too often, we compare ourselves to someone who we think is 'better' or has more; is more successful, has better skills and abilities or better looks and personal qualities, better or more resources and possessions, or has done more than you.

There's often someone who is more skilled, has more money, more happiness or whose children are cleverer than yours. There's usually someone you know of who got the opportunity that you had hoped for: the job, the free trip to Paris or the new partner. Comparing yourself with someone else – who they are and what they have – means you can only see what they've got and what you haven't. But negative comparisons can undermine your confidence, leaving you feeling inadequate.

Of course, it's natural to want to know where you fit into the scheme of things, but comparing what you don't have to what others do have will only make you miserable. Why would you want to make yourself miserable? You wouldn't do that to a friend; you wouldn't be unkind enough to point out to them the ways they don't match up and are less than others.

Ask yourself: 'How does comparing myself or my situation to others' make me feel?' If comparisons leave you feeling resentful, discouraged and feeling bad about yourself, then clearly it's not helpful to think like this.

So how can you be kinder to yourself? Start by being aware that comparing yourself to someone else puts the focus on the wrong person. Your skills, abilities, contributions and value are entirely unique to you. They can never be fairly compared to anyone else. So, compare yourself to yourself. Focus on what you've done and are doing rather than what everyone else has done and is doing. Reflect on what you've experienced, achieved and/or overcome.

Instead of comparing yourself with others, see them as role models to learn from and be inspired by. When we're inspired by others, we feel motivated to achieve and do well according to our own abilities, skills and resources. Being inspired means that you'll feel more positive and in control since you are no longer comparing what the other person has to what you haven't – you'll be too busy working towards what you want and what you can do.

Get things into perspective; compare less, appreciate more. Being more aware of what you do have rather than what, compared to others, you don't have, is a far more positive approach. Identify the good fortune, privileges and qualities you have and build on them.

Think positive

Being able to think more positively about yourself, other people and events can also help you be kinder to yourself when things go wrong. Allowing the negative thinking – the reproaching and berating – to overwhelm you only serves to stop you from moving forward.

We're all familiar with the inner critic; that little voice in our heads that's quick to judge and is ready with a put down or self-pity. Your inner advocate is the other, positive voice in your head: the one that defends you.

When your inner critic puts you down or is full of self-pity, your inner advocate steps in and presents a kinder, more gentle perspective on your behalf. While your inner critic is against you and unkind, your inner advocate is for you, it supports you. Your inner advocate is kind. Next time you realise you're berating yourself, ask your inner advocate: 'What do I need to do right now? Oh yes, that's right, self-compassion.' Put your hand on your heart and speak supportively and with kindness to yourself.

Try to be more aware of your own self-talk. More often than not, you won't even notice when you're thinking in negative ways; berating and reprimanding yourself. But when you do, ask yourself: 'In what way is it helpful for me to think like this? In what way am I being kind to myself?' In future, when you catch yourself thinking negatively, remind yourself that negative thinking and self-talk does not help you feel good about yourself and your abilities.

For example, if, after a period of time, you're still reproaching yourself for having failed an exam or an interview, ask yourself: 'In what way is thinking like this helpful?' Wallowing in 'I'm crap' isn't helpful. It's self-pity. Sure, you failed, you screwed up. Acknowledge that. You can then choose whether to dwell on it or move onto more positive, encouraging thoughts. Thoughts about what you can do to improve, to make a situation better.

Use this one simple rule: don't say anything to yourself that you wouldn't say to anyone else.

Have a phrase or word that stops the train of negative self-talk. If you find yourself slipping back into 'I'm crap. I'm hopeless', simply say 'Stop!' to yourself. Or tell yourself 'No, I'm not going there. I'm not thinking like that!' Then refocus your thoughts to more positive, helpful, kind thoughts and self-talk.

Anytime you do catch yourself saying a negative sentence, add the word 'but'. This prompts you to follow up with a positive sentence. How, for example, could you finish these sentences? 'I failed the interview *but* … ', 'I've upset someone *but* I can now … '.

Learn from your mistakes

If you've ever learnt to drive or learnt to play a musi-cal instrument or speak a foreign language, you'll know that as you went along you made mistakes. Maybe you misunderstood what you were meant to do or say or you miscalculated where and when you were meant to have done something.

But you learnt from those mistakes; you saw where you went wrong and practised until you got it right; became more adept, efficient and capable. So, you've dealt with mistakes before, you can do so again in other situations. You can't change mistakes, but you can choose how to respond to them; you can learn from them.

It can be so easy to fall into a negative spiral of self-pity and feeling sorry for ourselves. Very often we wait for self-pity, guilt, regret and so on to pass on their own without working to make ourselves feel better. Accept-ing defeat and giving up feels easy, because it takes less work than pulling ourselves out of a pit of despair.

But it *is* worth making the effort. You *can* make yourself feel better. Here's how.

Don't try and ignore or deny a mistake, but don't obsess about it either. Instead, acknowledge and accept that what's done is done and can't be changed. Look for the lessons. What did you learn? Rather than thinking, 'I should/shouldn't have', try saying 'I could/should have … *but* now I'm going to … ' or 'next time I'll … ', or 'it might help to ... ', or 'I could ... ', or 'now I'm going to ... '. If what you did or didn't do affected someone else, have you acknowledged what happened and apologised? It's important that you and the other person know that you're aware of the damage done and are clear on what, if anything, you can do to make amends. If, for some reason, it's not possible to apologise – the other person is no longer around or part of your life – write out your apology and imagine that you have been forgiven. Then move on.

Instead of blaming and berating yourself, think about what you learned from the experience. What matters is what you learned, what you do now and what you do next time a similar situation presents itself.

Tell yourself the *whole* story, not just one aspect. Remember to put what happened into perspective; understand how and why it happened, and see all that came out of it. See *everything* that has happened as a result of what you did or didn't do; not just the negative aspects, but also what lessons you learned from it.

Step outside yourself and see that what's happened is part of the grander scheme of things. One way to do this is to think about how you will view your mistake, what you did wrong or failed to achieve, a year from now; two years, five years. Acknowledge that you're continuing to grow into the person you're becoming, and that the person you are right now also deserves kindness.

Be kind to yourself! See yourself as a person of worth; doing the best you can with what you have.

You've done something wrong, yes, but you're still a good person. Think about what you would say to someone else in the same situation to make them feel better. Remember that you, too, deserve your own kindness and compassion. You also deserve forgiveness.

Forgiving yourself means no longer berating yourself. Instead, you accept what happened and find a way to move forward. Maybe you didn't say or do something and you wish you had? Perhaps you once smiled in implied assent to someone's racist or misogynistic comment when, actually, you should've challenged it. You may have missed a great opportunity because you hesitated for too long: a job or travel abroad. You wish you'd not dithered about it; now you keep thinking about what you missed out on.

Know that all the time you are unable to forgive yourself for something that happened days, weeks, months or even years ago, you are living in the past; you're letting the hurt and pain burden you by holding onto it. That's not kind!

Once again, think about what you would say to someone else in the same situation to make them feel better. What kind, helpful things would you say? How would you reassure them? What would you suggest they do?

Now, do that for yourself; show yourself kindness and compassion.

In a nutshell

- Berating and blaming yourself when you make a mistake or screw up or when you can't cope doesn't give you what you need most: kindness, hope and encouragement.
- It's important that you treat yourself kindly through all the ups and downs in your life; treat yourself like a lifelong friend, with the same kindness and care, respect and support you would give to someone that you care about.
- Self-pity can tip over into being self-absorbed and self-centred. Just as you can't help others from a position of judgment, you can't help yourself – or anyone else – when you're stuck in self-judgment and pity.
- Self-kindness and compassion do allow you to feel sad for yourself, but also encourage you to do something constructive to make things better; to improve your situation.
- Just like kindness to others, there's a number of aspects to self-kindness; aspects such as self-respect, empathy and perspective, courage, acceptance and patience, forgiveness, gratitude and appreciation.
- Self-respect means believing that you are good and worthy of being treated well – not just by other people, but by yourself too – even when you screw up,

make mistakes, don't achieve or do well in some area of your life.

- Empathising with yourself means seeing yourself from someone else's kindly perspective; responding to yourself with the same understanding as a good friend would give you for what you did or didn't do.
- Consider the circumstances at the time you made a mistake or did something wrong. Be kind to yourself; know that whatever it was you did or didn't do was based on conditions – what you knew or were able to do – at the time.
- Take responsibility – don't deny that you screwed up in some way. Accept what happened and what you did or didn't do. Nothing can change that. But what *can* change is what happens next. Learn from it, act differently next time. And if your wrongdoing affected someone else, apologise. Then let it go.
- We've all got weaknesses and imperfections. Accept that in some things you're a bit crap. But more often than not, good enough is good enough, and even no good at all can be OK.
- You simply can't do and be anything and everything. Rather than berate yourself, accept yourself. There are things you don't like. You can accept that. Accept, too, that you're not skilled and perfect in some areas of your life. Just as likes and dislikes are part of who you are, so are your failings and foibles.
- Of course, if you want to, you can still do better. Acknowledge your potential and aim to improve, just one step at a time. Tell yourself: 'I am enough.

Tomorrow I can strive to be more, but right now, I'm enough.'

- Avoid the comparison trap. Comparing what you don't have to what others do have will only make you miserable. Why would you want to make yourself miserable? You wouldn't do that to a friend; you wouldn't be unkind enough to point out to them the ways they don't match up and are less than others.
- Instead of comparing yourself to others, see them as role models to learn from and be inspired by.
- Compare yourself to yourself. Focus on what you've done and are doing rather than what everyone else has done and is doing. Reflect on what you've experienced, achieved and/or overcome. Identify the good fortune, privileges and qualities you have and build on them.
- Acknowledge that you're continuing to grow into the person you're becoming. Know that you're a person of worth, doing the best you can with what you have.
- You may have done something wrong, but you're still a good person. What kind, helpful things would you say to a friend? How would you reassure them? What would you suggest they do? Now, do that for yourself; show yourself kindness, compassion and forgiveness.

7

Kindness When Your Life is Really Difficult

What, though, if you're facing something more serious than having screwed up, made a mistake, failed to achieve something, been unfair to someone else or some other wrongdoing?

Perhaps you recently lost something or someone you love: a bereavement or a relationship break-up or a close friend or family member has moved away. Perhaps you've lost your home or your job.

Maybe you've moved somewhere new and very different and you're struggling to adjust. Maybe you've become a parent for the first time and you're finding it difficult to cope. Or it could be that there was something you desperately wanted – a child, a qualification, a place on the team or a promotion – but didn't get.

Any of these things can knock you sideways and leave you feeling sad and lonely, anxious and vulnerable. So can caring long term for someone else – a child, your partner, a sibling or parent – with a physical or mental illness, or coping with your own physical or mental illness. So can incidents of discrimination, abuse or being bullied. Whatever the issue and the circumstances, the common experience is often a feeling of being disconnected; you feel sad and alone. You may feel cut off and isolated from others. Maybe you feel no one understands or that they misunderstand.

You need kindness and compassion.

Understanding sadness

In order to treat yourself kindly in these difficult situations, it helps to understand what's going on. It may be hard to believe, but feelings of sadness are there for a good reason. Sadness does have a positive intent. Its purpose is to slow down your mind and body to give you time to take in the new circumstances and accept that what has happened *has* happened. Nothing can change that. Yes, you might go over events and ask yourself 'What if … ?', 'Why didn't I … ? and 'I should have/they should have … '. Thoughts like these are part of the process of accepting what happened or is happening.

It's okay to be sad. You might think, 'I shouldn't be so upset. What's wrong with me?' But you need to accept sadness for what it is: a temporary and useful state that can help you adjust – to get used to changed, different circumstances – and to accommodate the changes and learn to live with them.

You may feel disconnected and disorientated. As the author C. S. Lewis noted after the death of his wife, 'At times it feels like being mildly drunk, or concussed. There is a sort of invisible blanket between the world and me. I find it hard to take in what anyone says.'

Whether you've been bereaved or suffered some other loss or major life change, be kind to yourself; don't expect too much of yourself, your mind needs time to catch up with and process the changes in your life – your new reality.

Sadness also conveys to others that you are experiencing loss or failure so that they can respond appropriately, with kindness and compassion, and give you time and space, comfort and support. So, treat yourself like a good friend – with the same kindness and care and support. Let yourself be sad. As writer and meditation teacher Susan Piver has said: 'Despair is what happens when you fight sadness. Compassion is what happens when you don't.'

Take the pressure off

When you're going through a tough period in your life, you need to prioritise your commitments and obligations so that you can slow down and adjust. Which of your commitments and obligations are not so important right now? Ask yourself questions such as: What do I want and not want? What do I want to do with my time? For now, what do I have to do and not have to do? Where do I want to go and not go? Who do I want to see and not want to see? Who depends on me? For now, what and who can I drop?

Take the pressure off. Reduce your commitments. It doesn't mean that you should cut yourself off from everything and everyone, but in tough, difficult periods of your life, self-care means being aware of your limits and, for now, sticking to them – saying 'no thanks' or 'not now' to requests for your time, for your presence, abilities and contributions.

When you're feeling overwhelmed, it's OK to say no. It's not selfish or unkind. When someone asks you to do something, makes a suggestion or extends a well-meaning invitation, notice how you immediately feel. Disinterested? Anxious? Pressured? Stressed?

Simply say 'Thank you but I don't want to/can't/don't feel up to it'. There's no need for a long explanation and excuses. Be honest; you only need one valid reason why you can't or don't want to do something. But do thank the other person for asking you and maybe offer a compromise – suggest they ask someone else or they ask you again next month.

However, although you need to step back from life for a while when you're going through a difficult period, don't drop all your connections with others. Your link to family and friends is important for your sense of well-being and belonging. You just need to tighten the circle for a bit and limit your time to spending it with those people who support or comfort you in some way.

It's easy to feel like few people, if any, care or understand what you're going through. Often, other people don't know what to do or say, so they do or say nothing. So, even though you're the one who's facing a tough time, you may need to be the one to get in touch.

Reach out to those you can trust; friends or family who will listen and comfort, who have a calm concern and won't try to judge or fix you. You might want to tell them how you've been feeling – confused, anxious, sad, angry, upset, exhausted – but if you find that some friends can't handle your feelings, that's OK. Everyone has their abilities and their limits. If a friend or family member is not able to listen or talk with you about how you're feeling, ask them to do something practical to help. Leave talking about how you feel to someone who is able to listen and talk with you about it. And whatever it is other people are able to do for you, do tell them you appreciate their concern or support.

Whatever your situation, there's information and support to be found from others that have been or are going through the same thing – being a new parent, coping with an off-the-rails teenager, a relationship break-up, redundancy, financial problems and so on. Talk to someone you know who's experienced the same difficulties or Google a local support group and helpline. You'll be able to talk to people who understand what you're going through, provide opportunities to share experiences, information and ideas on how to move on or feel better.

If, though, you have no one to talk to or feel that a helpline or support group isn't helpful, if you feel over-whelmed too often or for too long, then *do* go and speak with your doctor.

Indulge yourself with comfort and reassurance

Self-compassion isn't a 'poor me' feeling of self-pity; it's just recognising that sometimes life is very difficult and that you need to do things to make life easier. To a greater or lesser extent, you need to be self-indulgent; to allow yourself to take it easy. This isn't a bad thing. It means you are creating conditions that allow you to integrate what's happening – or what has happened – into your life.

It's hard to look forward to each day when you know you will be experiencing pain and sadness. So, each day decide to have something to look forward to. No mat-ter how small it is, have something you can do that you enjoy. Whether it's reading, baking, going for a walk, having lunch with a friend, singing – in a choir or on your own – gardening, doing a crossword, playing com-puter games; do whatever it is that you like to do.

Comfort yourself. Think of pleasant things you can do. Get a massage. Eat healthy comfort food. Wear a favourite piece of clothing. Have a warm bath or a hot shower. Hug or cuddle someone who loves you. Hold-ing hands or walking arm in arm with a friend or family member can comfort and reassure you.

Do something nice for someone else; a small kindness that will take your mind off what you're going through.

Watch an uplifting film, or funny pet videos on YouTube. Look at a book or website with beautiful scenery or beautiful art. Whatever brings you moments of pleasure.

Listen to music. Music can help you access a range of feelings: anger, sadness and happiness. Music can soothe or uplift you. Music that you find beautiful and uplifting can provide hope and encouragement – Flaming Lips 'Do You Realise', for example, or Elbow's 'One Day Like This'. Or for something more upbeat, Boston's 'More than a Feeling' or Fleetwood Mac's 'Don't Stop Thinking about Tomorrow' and Primal Scream's 'Moving On Up Now'. These are just songs which came immediately to my mind; of course, you'll have your own favourites from one or many genres of music – classical, jazz, country or folk, reggae, R&B and so on.

If you play an instrument or sing, then play that instrument or sing. If you have a hobby or passion that you can 'lose yourself' in, it can help you feel engaged and connected. Whatever it is that you get comfort and enjoyment out of, make yourself do it. Do something that gives you pleasure and comfort each and every day.

Doing things that you enjoy can help you move through sadness and difficulties, even if you don't initially feel like doing them.

There isn't one right way to take care of and be kind to yourself when you've been through a really difficult experience. When times are tough, what works for you might be different to what works for someone else. And what works for you today might be different from what helped a month ago, or what will help in a few months' time. Nothing stays the same – part of being kind to yourself is to be flexible. Again, treat yourself as you would treat someone else who'd suffered a loss or serious change in their life.

Moving on

At some point, the feelings of sadness, anger or upset that you are experiencing now will just be a sad memory. When you're ready, you can work towards that. However, when things are really difficult, when your situation is really tough, it can seem like nothing is going to change; that you won't be able to move on. You need a catalyst; something that will bring about a change. That catalyst is hope. Hope is an inherent aspect of kindness; hope encourages you to believe that things will eventually improve and be good and that you'll feel better.

With hope there is possibility. With hope there are alternatives. With hope there is help. Hope *is* help. Add hope to moments of comfort and enjoyment and you can start to move forward.

Create hope; visualise images for yourself – pictures where you are coping and things are going well. Imagine new possibilities. The more you imagine yourself coming out the other side, the more likely it is to happen. Your mind can create a world of possibility, in the present, which will give you hope for the future.

You will need to make a decision that you are going to move on. It won't happen automatically, you have to decide that you want to move forward, that you are going to think about how to move on and you are going to do it.

Have patience though; take things one step at a time. While it can be helpful to have goals to help you look to a brighter future, try to avoid rushing into things. Sometimes, in an effort to distract yourself and move forward, it's easy to make rash decisions: rush back to work, move home or jobs, break ties with people in your life or take on new relationships too quickly.

Is there anything that needs to be adjusted or changed in order to go forward? Be open to new ideas and ways of doing things. Think along the lines of 'It might help to … ', or 'I might try … ', or 'I could … ', or 'Now I'm going to … '.

Start making small changes that will help start a shift in your life and help you move on.

You could start by keeping an 'achievement journal'. Note the things, no matter how small, you achieve each day. When you're going through a difficult time in your life and are struggling to feel better, noting small achievements can help you to see that you can do things and you can build on those things to help you move on.

What gets included may depend on how you're feeling that day. Sometimes it might simply be that you got out of bed and got dressed. It might have been an effort to get out of bed and it was an achievement worth noting down. Sometimes it might be household chores or work tasks. There's a wide variety of things in our lives that make for small achievements. Maybe, for example, you sent an email to Sadiq, had a chat on the phone with Carrie, read a couple of chapters in a book, learned how to make French toast, listened to the news, cleaned the bathroom. Maybe today was the day you went out with friends for the first time in ages or you booked a holiday. Perhaps you returned to work.

Regularly write in an achievement journal and every now and then you'll be able to look back through it to reflect on all that you've learned and achieved. It will all add up to quite a lot of small achievements. You can also add those things that you feel grateful for – the things you appreciate.

Look for the positives. When life feels like it's weighing you down more than normal, it can seem like everything is wrong, bad or hopeless; there's nothing positive. But there are positives – you just have to look for them. Again, it might only be small things – this morning's coffee, hearing birds sing in your garden, a funny text from a friend, something good on TV – or it could be bigger things; maybe you have a good job, or a supportive boss, family, partner, neighbour or friend. Whatever, add them to the achievement journal.

Make a contribution. If you can help other people, in the process, you help yourself. You could sign up with a voluntary organisation or you could simply do something kind for a friend, family member, neighbour or colleague. Even helping just one person is a start. It will take the focus off yourself and your situation in the most positive of ways.

Expect, though, to have bad days. Weeks, months, over a year after a difficult time in your life, you might have a day or more when, although it feels like there is no reason at all to feel knocked back, you just are. If you're having a bad day, especially if it's after a period of better days, there's no need to wonder 'What's wrong with me?' Bad days do happen. They will pass. Accept that sometimes you have a bad day for an obvious reason and sometimes for no apparent reason. On those days, be kind and gentle with yourself. Phone a friend, stay in and eat pizza and have an early night. Or whatever works for you.

As the Austrian poet Rainer Maria Rilke said: 'Let everything happen to you: beauty and terror. Just keep going. No feeling is final.'

If, however, you're concerned that you're not able to move forward, do speak to your doctor.

Kindness when you're ill or injured

There's a wide range of circumstances – a bereavement or a relationship break-up, for example, or losing your home or your job, incidents of discrimination, abuse or being bullied – that can knock you sideways and leave you feeling sad and lonely, anxious and vulnerable. So, of course, can an injury or illness. None of us choose to get injured or be ill. But, to a certain extent, we can choose how we deal with it. Having an injury or being ill is *the* time to prioritise self-kindness; being gentle, good and easy with yourself.

If you work, call in sick. If you have social plans, cancel or reschedule. If there's housework to do, leave it. Rest is more important. Feel guilty? It's misplaced guilt; you're not doing anything wrong by doing what you can to get better. Time and energy you put into other things is time and energy diverted from you getting better. Your health is important, and in the long run you will be able to do more if you rest now, as it will speed up your recovery.

Any day that you're unwell, make sure you're comfortable. Wear comfy, loose clothes, curl up in bed or bring your duvet and pillows into the living room and make yourself comfortable on the sofa. Gather everything you need – medication, tissues, hot water bottle, books and magazines, laptop and phone and their chargers, the TV remote and anything else – into one place so you don't have to keep expending energy and effort getting up and down.

Being unwell is a time to do things that bring comfort and calm. Simple things like cuddling a hot water bottle or taking a long, hot bath. Re-read a favourite book or something new by a favourite author. Use this opportunity to catch up on some reading or that box set you've been meaning to watch. All of the little pleasures that you usually don't find time for can be enjoyed when you're unwell. There's nothing to feel guilty about – you're not doing anything wrong by indulging yourself in this way. Quite the opposite – you're doing everything right; you're being kind to yourself.

Eat healthily, but do also eat comfort food – soups and stews, hot buttered toast, pizza, macaroni cheese, hot chocolate – whatever you love. Don't, though, let food shopping sap your energy. Try to plan for everything you're likely to need for the next few days and either ask someone else to get it or do an online food order.

If you have children to take care of, know that you can't be Supermum or Superdad while you're feeling ill. Your children certainly won't hold it against you forever if you ditch the sports practice, craft activities and outdoor adventures for a few days and let them resort to TV and computer games. Will they? Give yourself – and them – a break.

And in the evening, when the children go to bed, if you're not already there, you go to bed. Don't use the evenings to get other stuff done. Your body imposes a curfew when you're ill – obey it or it will punish you the next day!

Let others take care of you

Let others know that you're unwell, via text, email or social media. Don't be boring and go on about it, but don't say you're fine when you're not. Don't say you don't want to be any trouble. Don't be a banana! Take help when it's offered. And if someone says 'let me know if I can do anything', think of something!

If they don't offer, then ask. Ask for help and support. Be specific about what it is that you'd like someone to do for you and ask them. Whether it's getting the washing off the line, walking the dog every day or making some phone calls on your behalf, let others help. Just as being ill is an opportunity to do things that bring you comfort, it's also a time to ask for and accept the care and help of others. So, if someone you trust is happy to help, just let them. Even if they don't do things exactly how you'd want them to be done, let go of perfection and accept that, right now, what they're doing and how is good enough.

Express your appreciation. Accepting help, expressing gratitude and appreciation, is a reminder of how both the person who's unwell and the person who helps and cares can benefit from the exchange of kindness.

Ease back into your life

As you start to feel better, it can be tempting to throw yourself back into your usual routine. But pushing yourself to take two steps forward could mean you then find yourself going three steps back. Even if you feel better, your body will be weak from the illness and your immune system needs to regain its strength. Know that energy you use up doing everyday things is energy diverted from getting better. Be kind to your body. Have patience, take it slowly – one step at a time.

Illness makes us slow down, so it's a good time to do the simple things. Things that don't take up too much time and energy.

Write a letter or email to someone you haven't caught up with in a while, go through old photos, declutter a cupboard, your wardrobe or a bookshelf. Small, simple tasks can seem like a chore when you're in the midst of a busy life, but when you're unwell those little tasks might provide the simplicity and the right pace for you and won't take much energy either.

You might also use the time to catch up on gestures of kindness to others – phone calls, emails, letters to friends or thank you notes.

Use the change of pace that illness or an injury brings to reflect on what you want to do when you do feel better. Sometimes, it's possible to trace back your illness to an imbalance in your life. Maybe you've been pushing yourself too hard, at work or in your family life? Maybe you've been overdoing it with junk food, alcohol, smoking or drugs? Maybe you've not been getting enough sleep or exercise? Maybe you sustained an injury because you were rushing or taking short cuts with something?

Too often, when we tip the balance we risk being overwhelmed and then falling ill or getting injured. Illness and injury can be a wake-up call to value your health and redress the balance.

In a nutshell

- A serious loss or a major change in your life can knock you sideways and leave you feeling sad and lonely, anxious and vulnerable. You need kindness and compassion.
- It's okay to be sad. You might think, 'I shouldn't be so upset. What's wrong with me?' See sadness for what it is: a temporary and useful state that can help you adjust – to get used to changed, different circumstances – and to accommodate the changes and learn to live with them.
- Sadness also conveys to others that you are experiencing loss or failure so that they can respond appropriately, with kindness and compassion, and give you time and space, comfort and support.
- Treat yourself like a good friend – with the same kindness and care and support.
- Take the pressure off. Reduce your commitments. In difficult periods of your life, self-care means being aware of your limits and, for now, sticking to them; saying 'no thanks' or 'not now' to requests for your time, presence, abilities and contributions.

- Don't, though, drop all your connections with others. Your link to family and friends is important for your sense of well-being and belonging.
- Google a relevant support group and/or helpline. You'll be able to talk to people who understand what you're going through, who can provide opportunities to share experiences, information and ideas on how to move on or feel better.
- If a friend or family member isn't able to listen or talk with you about how you're feeling, ask them to do something practical to help. Leave talking about how you feel to someone who *is* able to listen and talk; to offer comfort, sympathy and reassurance.
- Whatever it is other people are able to do for you, do tell them you appreciate their concern or support.
- It's hard to look forward to each day when you know you will be experiencing pain and sadness. So, each day decide to have something to look forward to. No matter how small it is, have something you can do that you enjoy and that brings you a small comfort.
- Add hope to moments of comfort and enjoyment and you can start to move forward. It won't happen automatically, you have to decide that you want to move forward, that you are going to think about how to move on, and you are going to do it.
- While it can be helpful to have goals to help you look to a brighter future, try to avoid rushing into things. Be open to new ideas and ways of doing things. Think along the lines of 'It might help

to … ', or 'I might try … ', or 'I could … ' or 'Now I'm going to … '.

- Try keeping an 'achievement journal'. Note the things, no matter how small, you achieve each day. You can also add those things that you feel grateful for – the things you appreciate.
- Expect to still have bad days. They will pass. Accept that sometimes you can have a bad day for an obvious reason and sometimes for no apparent reason. On those days, be kind and gentle with yourself.
- None of us choose to get injured or be ill. But, to a certain extent, we can choose how we deal with it. Having an injury or being ill is *the* time to prioritise self-kindness; being gentle, good and easy with yourself.
- Time and energy you put into other things is time and energy diverted from you getting better. Your health is important, and in the long run you will be able to do more if you rest now, as it will speed up your recovery.
- Any day that you're unwell, do simple things that bring comfort and calm. Take help when it's offered. If someone says 'let me know if I can do anything', think of something! If they don't offer, then ask. Be specific about what it is that you'd like someone to do for you and then ask them.
- Even when you feel better, your body will be weak from the illness and your immune system needs to regain its strength. Know that energy you use up doing everyday things is energy diverted from getting better. Be kind to your body. Have patience, take it slowly, one step at a time.

- Sometimes, it's possible to trace back your situation to an imbalance in your life. Illness and injury can be a wake-up call to value your health and redress the balance.

8
Feel Good About Yourself

I used to put my welcome mat the wrong way round so the world felt more inviting.

Morgan Rees

Identify and acknowledge your strengths

Too often, we focus on what we're no good at and the things we don't do well. But there are always going to be things we can't do, things we can't be; there are always going to be mistakes that we make. Of course, there's nothing wrong with wanting to put right a wrong, to do better, to be aware of your potential and aim to improve, but being preoccupied with what's 'wrong' and trying to fix it is an uphill struggle. Cut yourself some slack! Give yourself some recognition; identify what you do well – your skills, qualities and strengths.

Your strengths are the personal qualities, abilities, knowledge and skills you already have. Read through this list and, as you do, tick any quality that you think is true of you.

Adaptable	Good natured ✓	Persistent
Adventurous	Hardworking ✓	Practical
Calm	Helpful ✓	Precise
Caring ·	Honest ✓	Realistic
Cooperative ··	Imaginative	Reassuring ✓
Conscientious ✓	Independent	Reliable ✓
Courteous ✓	Innovative	Resilient
Creative	Intuitive ✓	Resourceful
Curious	Likeable ✓	Responsible ✓
Decisive	Logical	Sense of humour
Dependable ✓	Loyal ✓	Sincere ✓
Determined	Methodical	Sociable
Diplomatic ✓	Meticulous	Sympathetic ✓
Empathic ✓	Objective	Tactful ✓
Encouraging ✓	Observant ✓	Thorough
Energetic	Open minded ✓	Tidy
Fair ✓	Optimistic	Tolerant ✓
Firm	Organised	Trustworthy ✓
Flexible	Outgoing	Truthful ✓
Friendly ✓	Patient	Understanding ✓
Gentle ✓	Perceptive ✓	

Now choose your top five qualities; the five that you think most describe you. Then, for each quality, write a sentence or two that describes how and why you are like this.

For example, if you felt that being organised was one of your qualities, you might say: 'I arrange things in a logical order; I know what, where and when everything is. I can create order out of disorder and chaos!'

If another one of your qualities was that you were tactful, you might say: 'In potentially sensitive situations I know how to be honest while, at the same time, avoid giving offence.'

And if being reliable was one of your qualities, you might have written: 'I can be trusted and depended on to do what I say I will.'

For each of the five qualities, think of an example when you have used that quality – when you've got things organised, been tactful, been reliable. If you have difficulty identifying and coming up with examples of your qualities, ask someone you trust to help you. They'll come up with things you might not see in yourself. By identifying your attributes – your qualities and skills – and thinking about how, why and when you have each quality, you're creating your own personal affirmations; positive truths about yourself.

As well as your strengths and qualities, acknowledge things you're good at; your skills – skills you've acquired through work, study, hobbies and interests. Add something you like about your physical appearance as well.

Get into the habit of identifying and thinking positive things about yourself and create your own personal affirmations. Write them down and keep them where you can read them as and when you need to.

Recognise your efforts and achievements

Think of the last time you achieved something. Maybe you finished a difficult project or learnt something new? Perhaps you passed a test or exam? Maybe you finally got round to completing some small task you'd been putting off for ages – sorting out the cutlery drawer or cleaning out the fridge?

Of course, achievements come in all shapes and sizes, but whatever it was, did you take the time to acknowledge your achievement or did you simply move on to the next thing without stopping to reflect and congratulate yourself? Acknowledging your achievements, even in a small way, increases your self-respect, happiness and confidence. It's being kind to yourself!

Be more aware of your own achievements and give yourself recognition. When you do something you're pleased about, stop for a minute and recognise it. Compliment yourself; tell yourself, 'Good for me! I've done OK.' Or, 'That went well, I'm pleased with myself.' Or 'All that effort paid off. Well done me!' Or 'Hurrah! I'm brilliant!'

Take a compliment

As well as recognising your positive qualities, skills and achievements, another way you can be kind to yourself is to appreciate a compliment. If someone gives you a compliment, do you accept it and allow it to make you feel good? Or, do you brush it off? Perhaps you don't want to appear immodest or the compliment or praise doesn't line up with how you see yourself. But when someone gives you a compliment, it's like they are giving you a gift. Therefore, if you reject the compliment, it's like rejecting and refusing to accept a gift. And that's not nice, is it? It's not nice and it's not being kind to yourself or to the other person.

Decide to accept what the person is saying as a real possibility; that it is possible that you look great, what you're wearing is lovely, that you have been helpful, that you do something really well, that you're clever, or whatever it is the other person has said as a compliment to you.

Believe the other person; they're being nice and they're being genuine. Aren't they? Be gracious; accept a compliment in the same way you would accept a gift; just say 'thank you'. And if you say more than that, make sure it's positive; say 'How nice, thank you'. Or, 'Thank you. I really appreciate you telling me.'

Do more of what you enjoy

People with self-kindness are constantly recharging their batteries; they know their limits and know that they need to take care of themselves: to get enough sleep, eat healthily, find a way to reduce and manage stress and, whatever their abilities, get some form of daily exercise. And, just as importantly, they do things they enjoy.

You too can do the same; sleep and eat well, exercise and manage stress. And every day – or as often as possible – give yourself a small treat; give yourself a small kindness. It could be something enjoyable to read, listen to or watch. It could be something good to eat or drink, something to do – a hobby, an interest, a class or a club. Make time to do something that you enjoy: creative activities – art, crafts, writing; sports – walking, running yoga, pilates, or anything else that you love to do. Plan, too, for bigger things to look forward to – a day or a night out with friends, a weekend away, a holiday or an adventure.

If you see something that you really want, treat yourself. If it's expensive, save up for it. You don't have to wait for someone else to give it to you as a gift. Give it to yourself. And if the assistant asks 'Is it a gift?', say yes.

Make an effort to avoid the things, issues and people that bring you down. Know the things that leave you feeling bad about yourself and the world: the news, celebrity magazines and some social media websites. Limit their role in your life. Instead, read, listen to or watch media that uplift you. Read websites such as www.dailygood. org, www.huffingtonpost.com/good-news, www.good newsnetwork.org, for positive news stories and inspiring examples of other people's kindness.

Don't just read about positive people; search them out and spend time with them: colleagues, friends or family whose company you enjoy, who you have fun with. As far as possible, reduce the amount of time you spend with negative people who drain you and increase the amount of time you spend with the positive people in your life.

Gratitude

Get into the habit of identifying and reflecting on everyday small pleasures. The smallest things can make a difference to how you feel about your day.

Before you go to bed each night, identify three good things that have happened during the day. You could write them down in a notebook, or you may simply reflect on what those things are while you are brushing your teeth.

Maybe you had something really good to eat today, the train arrived on time and you received a humorous text from a friend. Perhaps it poured with rain but you remembered to bring an umbrella with you, someone else cooked dinner and you watched something brilliant on TV. Or it could just be that the sun shone, your dog did something that made you laugh and you had a good hair day. Or you managed to fix something: a doorknob in the house or a knot in a necklace.

Just make an effort for a couple of weeks to identify the good things in your day. You will soon find yourself actively looking for things to appreciate and, after a while, it will become second nature.

Appreciate just knowing that you had good in your day so that, whatever else happened, you know that it did in fact have things that made it all worthwhile. And know, too, that reminding yourself of the good things that happened is being kind to yourself!

In a nutshell

- Identify and acknowledge your strengths: the personal qualities, abilities, knowledge and skills you have. Add something you like about your physical appearance as well.
- If you have difficulty identifying and coming up with examples of your qualities, ask someone you trust to be honest. They'll come up with things you might not see in yourself.
- Get into the habit of identifying and thinking of positive things about yourself and create your own personal affirmations. Write them down and keep them where you can read them as and when you need to.
- Recognise your efforts and achievements. Compliment yourself; tell yourself, 'Good for me! I've done OK.' Or, 'That went well, I'm pleased with myself.' Or 'Hurrah! I'm brilliant!'
- Accept a compliment in the same way you would accept a gift; just say 'thank you'.
- Do more of what you enjoy. As often as possible give yourself a small treat; a small kindness. Plan, too, for bigger things to look forward to. And if you see something that you really want, treat yourself. If it's expensive, save up for it.
- Avoid the things, issues and people that bring you down; that leave you feeling bad about yourself and

the world: the news, celebrity magazines and some social media websites. Limit their role in your life. Instead, read, listen to or watch media that uplift you; positive news stories and inspiring examples of other people's kindness.

- Don't just read about positive people; search them out and spend time with them: colleagues, friends or family whose company you enjoy, who you have fun with.

- Before you go to bed each night, identify three good things that have happened during the day. Reflecting on the smallest things can make a big difference to the end of your day.

Useful Websites

Mentoring and befriending

Age UK works to support and enable older people. Be a volunteer befriender – either in your community or by phone – to an elderly person. www.ageuk.org.uk/get-involved/volunteer/community-befriender/

Mencap's advocacy service enables people with a learning disability to speak up and make decisions about things that are important to them, while their Empower Me service provides personalised advocacy support for people with a learning disability. For volunteer opportunities go to www.mencap.org.uk/get-involved/volunteering

The Prince's Trust is a youth charity that helps young people aged 11 to 30 get into jobs, education and training. Be an e-mentor with The Prince's Trust. www.princes-trust.org.uk/support-our-work/volunteer

The Refugee Council exists to support refugees arriving in the UK; to ensure that they are treated fairly and with dignity, to enable them to find protection, and to help them rebuild their lives. They have a range of opportunities to support refugees. www.refugeecouncil.org.uk

Information to support a friend struggling with mental health

    Time to Change is a social movement changing how we all think about and act on mental health. For information to help support a friend or family member, go to www.time-to-change.org.uk/blog/how-help-friend-who-struggling-their-mental-health

    MIND is a mental health charity, concerned with making sure no one has to face a mental health problem alone. They can provide information and support to help you support a friend or family member. For more information go to www.mind.co.uk

About the Author

Gill Hasson is a teacher, trainer and writer. She has 20 years' experience in the area of personal development. Her expertise is in the areas of confidence and self-esteem, communication skills, assertiveness and resilience.

Gill delivers teaching and training for educational organisations, voluntary and business organisations, and the public sector.

Gill is the author of the bestselling *Mindfulness* and *Emotional Intelligence* plus other books on the subjects of dealing with difficult people, resilience, communication skills and assertiveness.

Gill's particular interest and motivation is in helping people to realise their potential, to live their best life! You can contact Gill via her website www.gillhasson.co.uk or email her at gillhasson@btinternet.com.

Index